Thank you to my amazing wife and girls.
You are my muse. Then there's Life,
you keep me humble and entertained.

A Voice at the Table

Contents

Forward

As Brendan's wife of over 31 years, I can honestly say we, as a couple, have benefitted from all his leadership training. Although we shape our lives through the lens of creativity and fun, there is also that element of "business." We are co-leaders/managers of everything from dinner prep to how we handle (or not handle) our adult children's concerns.

I always knew Brendan was passionate about helping others, I could see it in the way he lights up after anonymously donating to charities, in the way he takes on extra projects at work, and with his artistic endeavors how he will often gift his handmade leather pieces or an award-winning framed photograph. So, when I read through this book and realized how generous he was in sharing his decades of knowledge, I shouldn't have been surprised.

Can someone really be a "master" at something? There is always something more to learn, and in Brendan's case, just when I thought OMG, don't you know enough about leadership already, why are you taking another course – I realized that passion absolutely plays a role in his expertise. It comes out in his writing, how well he knows and is passionate about this subject, and yet he still continues to learn more.

Thinking "A Voice at the Table" was going to be a bit of a bore to me since I am not involved at all in the corporate sector for work, I was delighted not only to be entertained and moved, but also to be inspired to take a handful of what I've learned and apply it to my field of work and relations with others.

Deeann Kelly
Health Educator,
And wife of 31 years

"The way a team plays as a whole determines its success. You may have the greatest bunch of individual stars in the world, but if they don't play together, the club won't be worth a dime."   Babe Ruth

Chapter 1
Play Nicely Together

That is a wonderful quote from the Big Bambino. It holds true for all types of teams. Whether it's a sports team, corporate teams or a medical team. How we work together matters in so many ways, some you may not realize until you find yourself scrambling to get things done alone. I remember, and you may too, hearing my elementary school teachers shouting out across the playground "You kids play nice together!" Sometimes there was an "or else" attached to the end. Little did I know then that those five words would be so powerful and establish a foundation for what we crazy adults call collaboration.

We are meant to work together in some sort of choreographed process. None of us are in it alone, life that is, which includes our work life too. Ask any successful person and they'll tell you they didn't achieve what they did alone. It took a team. One person may have had that million-dollar idea, but from there it took collaboration and for us to play nice together. That doesn't mean there weren't disagreements and temporary silent treatments. To have achieved that success, participating parties eventually had to come together, talk it out and respect one another's opinion, then agree upon next steps to move forward.

Teamstage.com shared some great stats on this topic (Teamwork Statistics: Importance of Collaboration in 2023). One of them is that "99.1% of employees want to be part of an organization that nourishes honest communication." Meanwhile, "only 5.9% of organizations are in the habit of communicating their goals on a daily basis." A little bit of a disconnect there. Collaborative communication must feed from the top down and back up seamlessly.

As a professional After-Action Review Administrator, I have the honor of working with many people from different backgrounds, with different specialties and yes, different perspectives, which I do enjoy. I feel I am always learning something new. With this comes the need to sometimes ask the questions no one wants to ask, the hard questions and "the why " to clarify mistakes or even poor planning. It's not about finger pointing or putting anyone on the spot. I have an obligation to uncover "the why " for certain actions or the lack thereof. That can make people uncomfortable, no matter how hard I try to make the AAR space one of respect, openness and safety.

99% of the time people are very open to sharing and happy to have me assist them in discovering the lessons learned. The other 1%, are often stuck in their ways, don't see or understand the big picture and strategy to move forward. Sometimes this is due to the lack of communication within an organization. I have discovered that the 1% can be hesitant to be vulnerable, occasionally ego has put up a roadblock or fear of the unknown. The old saying "you are only as strong as your weakest link" is legitimately true. Not saying that the 1% mentioned are our weak links, but their actions, lack of action and ego can be a weakness in our chain. For the organization to achieve real success each significant link has to be operating at full capacity and working together. I like helping to bridge that gap between the 99% and 1% or any parties that have different perspectives. It is a passion of mine.

"Employees who worked collaboratively were 64% more likely to stick to their assigned task than their solitary peers. In addition, people who engaged in collaboration at work also reported higher levels of engagement, higher success rates, and decreased fatigue levels." Per an article on Zippia.com by E. Boskamp (2/2023). When we respectfully collaborate with one another in the workplace we can potentially eliminate pointless gossip, complaints about who did or didn't do what and most importantly we free our minds of diving into a rabbit hole of annoyance and anger.

This is why I love the AAR. It allows for all participants to have a voice and share their perspective, if they wish to do so, I never force anyone to talk. For all of us to play nice together we must understand one another's perspective, understand each other's why. We can all still have our own unique views and ideas. However, we have reached, or better yet, we have achieved an open and respectful platform in which to build and grow upon. As adults, we have learned to play nice together. That is when the team comes into its own and begins to feed off one another and excel. We all know our roles and responsibilities and take ownership, pride in what we do and how it connects with our fellow Team Members down the hall, in the next building and around the world. I like to share my "Three C's" with people (see figure 3). I find it to be the answer to many of questions, concerns, misunderstandings and uncertainties that take place not only in the workforce, but in life too. My "Three C's" are Communication, Communication and Communication.

Figure 3

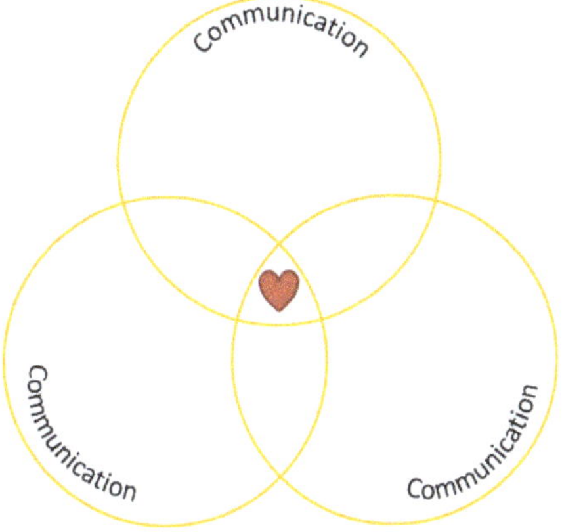

Within the heart of my "Three C's" is understanding, trust, clarity, accountability and knowledge, plus so much more. Being a good communicator takes practice and we learn as we go. I've been married to my lovely wife for over thirty years and I am still learning how to be a better communicator. Slowly, I am improving upon my grunts and ughs. Learning to speak real words. LOL.

One more thing I must add in here, if we are to play nice together, we must know when to stay in our lanes and when not to. Speaking with one of my best friends over a good cigar, he shared how lately some of his company's Team Members have been stepping out of their lane of responsibility and it was leading to client confusion and miscommunication. He and the owner had to have some heart-to-heart conversations and remind all Team Members of their roles and responsibilities. What to do if a client asks them something that is not part of their job function and if they go making changes without approval from higher up it'll be on their dime, not the company's.

This is not about them being hard asses and saying it's our way or the highway. It is about knowing your role, executing your job and understanding when to defer to a higher authority. Communication is the key. Don't talk about something you do not fully know and/or understand. Clients/customers will always try and get the best deal and if confusing a crew member and getting some extra stuff out it works, then they'll do it. We all love freebees.

Staying in your lane is important to all roles, it is how we depend on one another to do what is needed. Unless you are doing some extra assigned work, job training with a training supervision or preventing a serious

issue and emergency from taking place, just do your job
and do it to the best of your ability. Don't give answers or
suggestions to problems or issues you're unaware of. If you
desire to learn more and learn about other positions, ask
your supervisor for that opportunity to learn.
Communicating openly and respectfully is the foundation
to playing nice together.

"Teach yourself by your own mistakes."
William Faulkner

Chapter 2
Some Lessons I've Learned

As a little boy I was spazzy, curious, full of energy and most of the time I didn't think too much about what was going to happen next. I lived in the moment as most kids do. It was fun being a kid. Mostly because I didn't have to be an adult and do adulting things. Danger or off limits equaled an opportunity at some real fun in my mind (even through a chunk of my adulting years).

Years later I realized why I was that way. I remember thinking as a kid that I was a nobody. We were poor. A single mother household with three kids on welfare. In my mind I lived for the moment because the world didn't care about people from my social class/environment. I was teased for not having the newest clothes or for being the strange new kid in a new town every couple years. I had a minor speech impediment, for the longest time I got my "R's" and "W's" all messed up. The other kids took that bate and were relentless. Growing up in small towns and communities people knew everyone's business. People knew more about what was going on in my house than I did. I could see parents of the other kids talking and pointing and I thought nothing of it, or so I told myself.

This is not a woe is me tale though. This is what it is and how I personally have learned from those experiences, as well as the ones I share. For me, it is a reminder to be kind to myself. Some of the biggest bullies in our lives are us. We belittle, teardown, and criticize ourselves more than anyone else. We second guess ourselves far too much, which leads to us getting annoyed about it and the viscous circle of self-bullying goes round and round.

One of my earliest memories of realizing life wasn't all fun and games, was when I had to repeat first grade. Knowing what I know now, I was condemning myself and self-accepting that I was dumb and not worthy of being classified as a smart kid or one with potential. Trust me, it takes some serious work to fail first grade, but I managed to achieve just that. I didn't fail first grade due to the lack of knowledge gained. Nor did I have a crummy teacher, Mrs. Michaels was quite awesome. I can't blame my social/family situation. While it may not have helped, it wasn't the cause.

I failed first grade because I didn't do the work properly or I did a half-ass job so I could turn in the sheet and get out to recess where the fun was, which resulted in receiving bad grades. I remember being given worksheets with addition and subtraction problems and all I had to do was put the correct answer in a little square box under the problem. The only mistake I can remember Mrs. Michaels making is saying "Students, once you have completed your worksheet place it in the basket on my desk and then you may go out to recess."

What I heard was "get that worksheet in the basket as soon as possible and can leave this boring classroom and get to go outside and play." I knew five plus seven equaled eleven - just kidding it's twelve - but I had to get outside and play. It was my priority. Not understanding that my strategic placement of numerical drawings into small boxes had repercussions, had little to do with my understanding of addition and subtraction. If Mrs. Michaels would have added in "ensure you do your best work and if you get all of them correct you can go outside and play," then I would have done just that. I needed the right focus words. Plus, I didn't understand the why for things.

When the school year ended, and I had my final report card in hand, I saw a checkmark in the box that read "Must repeat first grade." It didn't really sink in at that moment. "OK, I get to play more with my friends and get down to some amazing recess time" was my thinking. When next year rolled around, I learned my friends that I had so much fun with during recess were now on a different schedule. Worse still, they were in an entirely different building. That's when it sank in completely. "I flubbed up!" First life lesson learned, you have to put in the work and understand the "why" for things.

My second year of first grade was much more productive. Not only did I complete the worksheets, but my numerical drawings were also the correct ones for the questions asked. Don't get me totally wrong though, I still wanted to get outside and play. I made new friends, and occasionally saw my old ones, but I understood what I had to do so I could move on to second grade. I was still spazzy, curious and didn't think much about what was next.

Fast forward to high school and I nearly, well kind of did, slipped into my old first grade habits. Perhaps still a bit spazzy, most definitely still curious, and future planning still wasn't a well-developed skill. I skipped classes to go skateboarding around town and to have fun. I wasn't a bad student, I got mostly A's when I did the homework and turned it in. I didn't cause trouble in class or school, and I had friends in all the high school social settings. I played sports in school and in community leagues and occasionally had girlfriends – though I must admit girls seemed like more of a drag than an asset at the time. I even worked during my high school years. Heck, I worked during my junior high school years. Delivering newspapers seven days a week, regardless of weather, and waking up double-dog early to get it done before school. I spent most of my high school years working at Dairy Queen. I simply connected earning money to being able to have more fun.

With the memories of two years of first grade far behind me, I gradually slipped back into a "fun first and then current responsibilities" both mentality and with my outlook. High school was a responsibility I had to take care of. In my senior year I switched high schools, buckled down and achieved mostly A's and was a model student. I even somehow became class president, which gave me the power to control, or at least have more input into, how students could have more fun.

Along the way I could have easily blamed the school counselors and teachers for not pushing me, not meeting one on one with me to understand me and help me to see the path I was on. Realistically they didn't have the time or didn't want to give their precious time to a student like me, when they could focus on the students with a bright future, the college-bound kids, that would help pad their school stats. The good students. It makes me laugh looking back; little did those teachers and counselors know that those good students did more drugs and drank more alcohol than I ever thought of.

The only complaint I had, and wondered quite often about, was why my mom was the way she was and why we had to be poor and live in the ghetto. As if we had a choice. "You can choose to be poor and live in the ghetto or select this lovely house with private rooms for all and have plenty to eat, stocked cupboards, full refrigerators and your mom will guide you through life. Time to choose, what will it be…?" I was a kid and didn't know the why. Plus, I never asked. It was part of my life and somewhere along the way I accepted it.

If I had asked why, and if my mom would have been open to sharing back then, I would have understood. I learned late in my senior year of high school that my mom was a drug addict. She was addicted to powerful prescription drugs. Some she received due to previous illnesses, playing the doctors like a violin, and others she stole from the hospital where she worked at the time.

"Why the drugs mom? Why?" I should have asked. If I would have asked I would have learned sooner that my mom was abused by her mom as a child. She had polio as a child and was still abused before and after. Her lifeline, the most important person to her at the time, wasn't allowed to see her, her dad. Therefore, there was no help coming from that source. I can well imagine the despair she was going through.

Her escape came at a young age, marrying my dad and having three children with him. My sister, brother and I make three, they are six and five years older than me. Her escape and so-called opportunity at a real life came to an end when my dad left her for another woman right before I was born. She was a single mother of three little kids, with only a high school diploma and an ex-husband that didn't help.

I now understand the "why", and when I began to understand I was able to put a lot of puzzle pieces together and see a much clearer picture. I could not complain. I was thankful for having a mother that busted her ass to provide the best she could for her three little kids.

What is impressive is that along the way my mom earned her nursing degree. She never stopped fighting the addiction and eventually overcame it. Sadly, the damage had been done. I lost my mom at the young age of sixty-six. She had the softest skin, most loving eyes and wanted the best for her kids.

I learned there is more to the story, there is a why for the actions we see and the ones we don't.

Though I had learned a lot in school, even if my teachers didn't realize it, the most educational and life changing time of my life came when I chose to join the U.S. Army. I had never thought about doing it. I just decided one day I had to get out of and away from Sacramento and all the people that were not adding anything positive to my life. My family was driving me crazy, so-called friends weren't really friends. Their idea of fun was drinking, drugs and sex. Perhaps we should have started a rock band? Looking back, it was my escape plan and I took it. I grabbed documents that I thought I might need to prove anything to the military and then some, jumped in my beat-up spray-painted VW Bug, and cruised to a recruiting office – after I looked in the yellow pages to find out where one was. I entered the building and walked in the first door on the right, which happened to be the Army. "How can I help you?" asked a man in uniform and I replied, "I'm here to join." Ten days later I was heading to basic training at Fort Sill, Oklahoma.

I'm not going to dive into a long spiel about my time in the Army, which could be a book in itself. What I will say is that having served for just under twenty-two years, I learned a lot about people. From various ethnicities, cultural backgrounds, and religious beliefs. From broken homes, perfect homes, and everything between. Criminals, the so-called righteous and even the occasional truly virtuous individual. The military is a melting pot of people, and it is a great opportunity to learn about them and listen to their "why." You'll hear every story imaginable, and you learn why they have the perspective they do on things.

What is even cooler, is that we manage to come together and work to achieve a common goal, and if we're in combat, it's as simple as watching each other's asses so we can all go home eventually. Through my time in the Army I learned how to listen and communicate with others, it's not a skill I was trained on, but it is perhaps the most valuable thing I learned.

Some perks along the way were meeting my wife of thirty plus years, having three amazing daughters together and having some of the most loyal friends a person could have. I retired in April of 2010. A big thank you to my soulmate and babe Deeann, our amazing daughters and the handful of best damn friends I made along this journey. I am forever grateful for all you've done for me and continue to do.

So much more to share, but like I said, that could be a whole other book on its own. The good outweighed the bad, even though some of the bad was damn horrific. Along the way, I often battled my own demons. I was angry far too often and when I drank it was to become numb and feel nothing.

On October 21, 2016 I decided to call it a day. What I mean by that is I made the decision to kill myself. It would be my second and final attempt.

I do not fully remember the next two and half to three days. A thick black permanent marker has been used to redact that time frame. All I know is that I had officially hit the bottom. The rock bottom and I was a bit of a zombie when I realized where I was. I remember laying in my assigned bed, looking at the ceiling, and counting the pale grey tiles over and over again. Why? Well, at the time, it was better than accepting where I was and for what, I had to though, and I did. I finally accepted I was in a mental health ward due to suicide tendencies and thoughts, extreme PTSD and letting all this turn me into an angry person.

I spent two weeks in the Marin Hospital Mental Health wing. Then three months in a fulltime outpatient mental health program. I learned to deal with my demons. I learned to forgive myself. I learned to accept. I learned that it's OK to cry and scream. I learned that crying and screaming is much better than hitting walls or throwing and breaking things.

My family and friends were right there by my side, helping me through the process. Listening or giving me the needed space.

Looking back and knowing what I know now, that time in my life was necessary. It made me face my demons, the troubled thoughts and dreams, and it helped my loved ones understand the "why" for my issues. Why I was so angry and flew off the handle at times, for the littlest of reasons. Then I learned why. Why I needed to put in the work and move beyond this and choose to live a happy and fulfilling life.

I share these snapshots of time in my life and experiences so that you, the reader, can understand we all have a "why". There is a why to all of our actions or lack thereof. We are wired uniquely due to the life we have led and have been a part of. If we are to work together, and achieve something amazing together, then we need to all have a voice at the table. We need to be vulnerable and share our experiences, just as much as our expertise, when it is appropriate and relatable.

Each of our perspectives will be valuable and will help develop a better way forward. It does not matter what kind of work or life environment one may be in or come from. We each bring a unique perspective to the table. When we listen to and learn from one another, we grow together and discover a better way forward. Perhaps even more importantly, we gain some understanding.

Never let someone else's accomplishments, or lack thereof, distract you from sharing your insight and why. I've known Ivy League graduates who had a hard time folding their own laundry, let alone doing it. On the flip side, I know people who didn't graduate high school but are some of the best leaders I've worked with.

We are all just people, simple silly human beings, each of us consisting of the same elements, with unique experiences and we deal with life and all its fun adventures in different ways. We have our own perspective on life and that is 100% OK. I find it quite enjoyable, the fact that we are all so similar, yet so very different. Fascinating isn't it?

Even at my age and recognizing all of the success I've had in life I still find time to doubt myself, at times I am still my own biggest bully. In my current career, I know my job and how to excel at it. I am a subject matter expert when it comes to it. Not being arrogant, just confident in my skill set. But there are times, plenty of them, when I internally yell, cuss and get mad at myself for mistakes or anything else random that truly does not mean anything. Regardless of how small and insignificant they may be. The ones that no one else notices except me, those get to me the most. Why? Well, that's the million-dollar question. A recent and lovely example of my self-bullying took place when I first saw the job listing for the role I am currently in.

I remember when I first saw the job posting for the role I am currently in now, I got super excited and said to myself "I know that stuff inside and out and all around!" Then at the end of the position title was "Executive." I froze and immediately went to that negative place that takes up space in our minds. I thought that there is no way that I am executive material. I'm just a common bloke that just happens to know a bit about the After-Action Review process. I closed the tab on my computer and finished eating my lunch.

Dr. Marina Nani, has a wonderful article published on Rich Woman Magazine's website called "From Self-doubt to Self-awareness: What You Don't Know About Yourself?" (Feb. 28, 2023). She says "it's important to remember that self-doubt is not necessarily a reflection of reality. Your thoughts and feelings are not always accurate representations of the world around you. It's important to question your self-doubt and challenge its validity." This is something I had to learn to do. Our minds are amazing and powerful things and with that they can create some amazing and powerful falsities about ourselves.

Dr. Nani continues to say "The good news is that the brain has an incredible ability to change and adapt. With practice, you can learn to reframe negative thoughts and replace them with more positive ones. This is where questioning self-doubt, not the outcome, becomes crucial.

Instead of focusing on the outcome of a situation, focus on the process and what you can learn from it." Through my own experience of questioning my self-doubt and not bullying myself, putting forth the facts and validating my abilities I proved to myself, maybe even convinced myself that this job opportunity was not too big for me. In fact, it was made for me. I applied and here I am a year plus later, helping people and teams to discover lessons learned and how to improve what they do.

We all have our doubts about things. I doubt that'll work or this will ever get done, such as the freeway work taking place around the DFW area. Never ending. However, let's work on not doubting ourselves and our abilities. It's OK to talk to yourself and walk through the process to see if an opportunity or anything else is right for you. That's using your brain wisely. Just be kind and real with yourself. Saying "I'm not smart enough" or "No way I can do that" is not only self-doubt, but you are setting yourself up to be bullied by yourself.

There is a never-ending arm-wrestling match taking place in our heads, the rational thinking vs. the irrational thoughts. It can wear a person out! I would ask you to do your best, train yourself and make it a habit to pause during those matches and lay it out in black and white. The facts vs. the assumptions. The facts will always win in the end when you take time to think rationally and when you take the time to be kind to yourself. If we come to the conclusion that we truly do not know something, then we can explore new opportunities to learn and exercise our minds. Or, we can simply move on and be content with what we are doing and that's 100% OK.

As we learn and grow, move through life, we need to also take the time to have quiet peaceful moments with ourselves. It's taking the time to have your own personal After-Action Review (AAR) with yourself, something we'll learn more about in the come chapters. I like to do this self-reflection at the end of the week or after big projects I was a part of. I ask that you keep the focus on you. You cannot answer or assume why someone else did something. That's for another time to learn, when groups/teams meet for an AAR. This time is strictly for you. Taking this time allows you to do a few things:

- Ask yourself how was your week? Or, how well did you do?
- What went wrong or could have gone better? Why? What was missing or failed to happen? Why?
- What went right this week? Why? How can I build upon this success?
- If you had doubts as to your abilities, what are the facts? "I can't do that?" is not a fact. "I've never been trained on that task before" Is a fact.
- How can I better collaborate with my peers to use my skills to improve our work environment?
- What do I need to do next week to improve myself? Why? What will this new learning opportunity provide me?

These are only a few examples, you can ask yourself anything you want, just be kind to yourself and be factual.

Don't assume and get yourself worked up over things you have zero control over.

"The most difficult thing in life is to know yourself."
Thales

Chapter 3
Complete the Sentences

Before we jump into all the fun things and thoughts I will be sharing, I wanted to take time for you, yes you, to listen and learn from yourself. For us to succeed, to live a happy life, achieve our goals and dreams we must be able to understand and know ourselves. What is our unique "why?" How would we answer a few simple questions about ourselves, how would we complete our sentences? The first being:

"I am… ………………………………………"

For some of us each sentence may be long and for others it'll be short, perhaps only one word added to it. BAM!! Done. I found myself completing my sentences and then doing it again. Then I did it again. I am many things, so I think. But, at the end of the day I am me. I know me, at least I like to think I do. Then, looking at it from a different perspective, a new sentence to emerges. Such as:

"I will.."

Well, well, well, what now? How would you complete it now? I could simply list my goals, "I will succeed" I will. But in what? Life? Over the past few years I feel I've evolved, I'm sure we all have with everything tossed at us over the last handful of years. With everything that has taken place, I wonder if the new norm is uncertainty. I have had plenty of time to spend with myself to ponder such things. On a positive note, this has led to a better understanding of my wants and needs, as well as a commitment to growth and myself. Can we even sum up ourselves in one sentence? Our beliefs, desires, wants, and prayers can all be overwhelming when jumbled together.

Our thinking process at times can be like a revolving door. Thoughts coming in and out and spinning around in our head. Annoying us. Confusing us. Pissing us off and my favorite, crazy or obscure thoughts leading to more crazy and obscure thoughts. It's easy to go down that rabbit hole. But at some point, we need to stand up to ourselves and say enough.

We do need to complete our sentence, for ourselves, and not for anyone else. Success begins with awareness, an awareness of ourselves, an awareness of our environment, and then expanding our awareness beyond our limits. Subsequently, we'll realize that success comes from many sources and directions. Opening up ourselves to new ideas and new activities is a lovely way of expanding our awareness and therefore not restricting ourselves. So, maybe one of the sentences should be:

"I will not… ……………………………"

Perhaps then, I'd write "I will not limit myself." I've learned that the past, present, and future all play a role in our day. We are multidimensional, ever expanding, and growing. Damn life is cool! It took me a while to realize this and honestly to accept it. When you think about completing your sentence, think about your passions, what makes you happy, and then not only write it out, act on it little by little or bigger steps as you see fit, and finally, do your best to live it.

When we identify what we truly want out of life, our personal life, work life, educational goals and so on, we become more engaged in all aspects of it. Not waiting around for something to happen, we plan for and work towards making it happen. Much like me writing this book. It was once simply cool sounding words coming from my mouth. "I'm going to write and have a book published one day." Those I mentioned it to gave me their skeptical support. Looking back then, I can't blame them. I was not focused. I was all over the place as to what I wanted to do in all aspects of my life.

Once I finally reached a confident combination of well-being, maturity and focus I was looking at 50 years gone by. Not to say I didn't have my moments of well-being, maturity and focus throughout my life, but none of them were consistent. It was becoming consistent that gave me the confidence to not only complete my sentence, but to believe what I was saying and then to act on it.

Looking back on my life, thinking about school, work and the activities I participated in, I realized I was only temporarily completing my sentence, "I can do that." However, I would only do something to a point where I could say to myself, "Yup, did that." I wasn't wise enough at the time to know it wasn't a matter of if I can, but can I do it consistently for the duration of it. Whether it be school, sports, work or anything else. Little by little I began to better understand this about myself. I learned who I was and most importantly, I accepted myself. I learned from mistakes. I learned from other people's mistakes. I also took the necessary risks that I was not comfortable with, but I knew I had to in order to move forward. I began to challenge myself and I confidently believed in myself.

After you complete your sentence or sentences, don't beat yourself up if you go astray, it happens. We are all imperfect-perfect humans. Take time to reflect and understand why you did what you did. Learn from the moment and try again. Hell, it took me five decades to complete my sentence and I still ponder my actions and events that took place. Now, I'm just kinder to myself and I've learned a lot better thanks to a life full of experiences, good and bad, funny and sad.

I completed my sentences and I'm happy to share them with you. They are my foundational sentences. Ones that coincide with my own personal values and beliefs.

- I am a man of strong belief and filled with love.
- I will do the best I can to be proud of myself and my achievements.
- I will not treat myself bad nor allow others to place their negativity upon me.

Write them down, memorize them, make them your mantra and share them if you'd like. It's up to you and what you are comfortable with.

"You can't expect your employees to exceed the expectations of your customers if you don't exceed the employees' expectations of management."
Howard Schultz

Chapter 4
Why Team Members are not Engaged

It is easy to just say and define a mediocre Team Member or student as not being engaged, don't care, or they are simply checking the block and moving on. I've been guilty of this, but then I took the time to ask why. Why are they doing the bare minimum? Asking them why and then simply listen. Listening to not only what is being said, but how it is being said, the visual expressions and what is not being said. When I started doing this I began to learn and understand the why behind the actions or lack thereof. I heard many "Whys" during my time and some may be familiar and/or relatable to you.

- Nothing changes. Whether I get my work done sooner or later. If I arrive early or stay late, nothing changes.
- My pay doesn't change, regardless if I do a great job, bad job or just meet the standard. There's no accountability.
- I'm not a kiss-ass like other people are.
- My boss is clueless and doesn't even know their job.
- I'm smarter than others that have gotten promoted above/before me.
- There is no benefit for me to excel or do more than need be.

I've heard those excuses quite often and when time permits I like to learn more about why they believe this and I ask for factual known data. Not "I heard from…." or "I assumed…." Those kind of answers are fear based and come from a place of uncertainty in one's own abilities or belief in themselves. I say that because we all have some kind of extra baggage we're dealing with. Self-doubt, jealousy, fear of the unknown and so on. Those living a successful life, not just work, a truly fulfilling life, have come to learn that they are only limiting themselves by committing those kinds of self-inflicted internal wounds.

As an After-Action Review expert, I wanted to understand the why for the numerous Team Members I engage with. Why do they show up to work? Why do they perform as they do? I knew this vital information would help me to better help each person of the team and the organization as a whole. So, I did a deep dive, researching and learning the facts. I came across a March 2022 survey of employees in higher education conducted by Grant Thornton, listing that 59% of faculty and staff felt that their voices were not being heard. Seeing this statistic made me do a double take. If I had been asked to give a ballpark figure I may have said 30%, but not more than 40%. Having that figure be almost 60% was disappointing to me.

If a Team Member feels that they are not being heard, then a couple things will most likely happen. One, they'll resign and find an organization that will listen. Or two, they will settle into a rhythm of simply going through the motions, checking the block each day, doing nothing more or less than what they have to do. Is this wrong? Is it fair to call them a bad Team Member? Those questions are open to discussion and will garner a variety of perspectives. For me, I can understand why and how a Team Member settled into that groove. My hope though, is that with proactive leadership and empowerment of Team Members, those that are just going through the motions re-discover their voice and begin to share more. Begin to feel they are being heard and that working together as one team has a positive impact.

It takes work, time and consistency.

A consulting group spent some time on campus when I was with UNTHSC, and upon completion of their visit/analysis one of the challenges our organization is faced with is effective communication. Looking at our previous three years of employee's Gallup polls results; our lowest score was that our Team Members feel their voices are not being heard. Though, I must include this year's data has shown significant improvement. Our results reflect what previous polls from a variety of organizations have found.

Communication is a vital part of any process and a vital part of any organization that plans to be successful. To have quality communication, organizations, leaders and Team Members have to develop a level of professional trust amongst one another.

Like many things, clear and precise communication needs to become a habit and then it'll be the norm. This includes the sharing of information and experiences. In my research and from speaking with people on my campus I also learned our departments tend to work in their own silos. The sharing of information and best practices is far from the norm.

A Team Member can very well buy into what a particular department is doing but may not buy into what the organization is doing overall. A good example is in higher education, due to the silo's that the departments and teams work in. The science department will certainly have their own core values and mission statement which will differ compared to that of the business department. Each has bought into their department's mission, but not completely sold on the university as a whole. When this happens, we have partially engaged Team Members, but the dots are not connecting to share the big picture. The why is only clear at a lower level, segmented and the big overall why goes misunderstood or ignored.

Organizational leadership has to make it a point

to take time to hear all the voices in the workplace. Not just upper management and other senior leadership.

Those voices make up a small percentage and I would ask if they are sharing the voices of all their Team Members, not just leadership and management in their departments.

I had the honor of working for the Fairmont for a bit, then COVID hit and I think a good majority know how hard the hospitality industry was hit. Nonetheless, it was a great time for me. One of the wonderful things the Accor Hotel Group, parent company of the Fairmont, did was develop the "Heartist" program or theme. Each Team Member is a Heartist in the organization, a valuable member of the team. Part of that was having a Heart of the House Committee, which I was privileged to lead. This group included Heartists from all departments and levels. Hourly workers to salary, managers to house keepers and we all shared a united vision of improving work life for all Team Members.

The power of this group was that all voices from all aspects of the property were heard and listened to. We had actively engaged Team Members. They were empowered and believed that their voice was being heard. This helps to explain why the Fairmont Sonoma Mission Inn and Spa is such a fabulous property. Just like other Accor hotels, they gave all Team Members a voice at the table.

I'm not saying this process was perfect and 100% of leadership or Team Members bought into it. Like anything else it had flaws and we did some learning as we took steps forward and steps backwards.

The key thing was the majority were in it together and were willing to take those steps. The people that could not get on board or participate with an open mind worked their way out of a job. Its unfortunate, but that too is a part of life.

An author that I enjoy reading is Tom Rath. You may know of him if you've read and completed the Strengthsfinder assessment. He also co-wrote How Full is Your Bucket (2004) with his grandfather Donald O. Clifton, a wonderful book. He has a quote that I quite like, "The key to human development is building on who we already are." I share that quote because it is important to understand who we are, our values and beliefs, how life has shaped us and what we can bring to the table. We grow and learn throughout life and life in itself is a process of learning and growing.

Before we go labeling Team Members as not engaged or mediocre let's learn and listen to their why. You might find out that through the years they have tried to voice concerns or opinions, but it fell on deaf ears. Or, the reason they do not participate in your annual survey is that they do not have the information or access to technology. How often do you see a janitor or housekeeper carrying around a laptop or iPad? Many people in those roles have English as a second language and do not receive all the information. Which gets significantly filtered as it makes its way through the communication pipeline. Plus, are you allowing Team Members the time to complete these surveys on company time? If not, why? It is company related. We get what we put into it and providing access, information and an opportunity should be something we supply to our Team Members. It's part of giving them a voice and helping them to feel that their voice is being heard and it is appreciated.

Gallup.com shared a report called "State of the Global Workplace: 2022 Report" and one of the findings is "Global engagement and wellbeing remain stable, but not great" and next to this are some statistics. Such as, 21% of employees are engaged at work. Another one was that 33% of employees are thriving in their overall wellbeing. I am an optimist by nature, but stats such as these make me wonder and think out loud, "Is this supposed to be good news?" This is when the pessimism comes out in me and asks why aren't the other 79% of employees engaged? Why aren't the other 67% thriving and in their workplace?

According to the Gallup report these unengaged and non-thriving employees are "Living for the weekend," "watching the clock tick," "work is just a paycheck." These are the mantras of most global workers. If this is truly the case, I have to ask why again? Why? I fully understand there will always be a segment of the workforce that is simply checking the box, watching time pass and taking as many breaks as possible to get a break from their work space and environment. However, from my experience the majority of the workforce I have been a part of wants to work and work towards achieving or making something that's kick-ass.

During my military recruiting days, we had lecture after lecture (that's phrasing it kindly) as to why we were not achieving the results we should have achieved. We participated in these lectures even when we did achieve what we were supposed to achieve. I remember one month my office was the top dog in all of our region. My team was pumped up and we celebrated our achievement. The following Monday morning I had to attend a leaders meeting. During that meeting, along with my fellow recruiting leaders in the region, we were cussed out and accused of slacking. Not being loyal and not giving it 100%.

I remember sitting there and thinking what is going on? Who pissed in this cat's cereal bowl this morning? The next three hours had the same theme. For those three hours I turned off. Only spoke when asked a question and kept it short. When the meeting was over my boss asked me to wait a second and once the others had left he said "I need more from you and your team." That's it, that is all he said to me. I do not remember my respectful reply, but in my head, I said "Fudge you!"

I share that story as an example of how not to attempt to lead. I say attempt, because my boss at that time was not a leader, he was a disgruntled manager with zero people skills. Five months later he was removed from his position. He said it was an unexpected transfer. Those of us leading the right way knew the real reason.

I reflected on that time some years later with a friend that also knew this previous supervisor and had heard of similar experiences. I ask my friend, "What if I had stayed back after that meeting and spoke with him one-on-one. Asking him what's going on? Asking him how can I help, beyond the normal responsibilities that I already have?" We pondered that for a spell and we had many thoughts that boiled down to we'll never know. However, it was a lesson learned. I needed to speak up and ask the

"Why?" If not in a meeting, then make time for a one-on-one to better understand.

Leaders must engage with their Team Members and help the unengaged become engaged. Knowing there is a small percentage that will still only do what they have to do and give the best lip service. Being able to recognize the middle grouping of people that are starving for guidance and want to improve, but don't know how or are not inspired to is critical. The top tier Team Members will always strive for excellence, it's in their DNA, it's how they are wired. With them, we can provide an idea or plan and they'll take the ball and run with it. This is what we call "Moving the Middle," it is nothing new or revolutionary, it's strategic thinking.

There are a handful of good books and articles on the subject of moving the middle. This "middle" area is untapped and full of potential, filled with team members wanting and waiting to excel. All they need is a bit of encouragement, a purpose they can get behind, some clear direction and they'll take off. We shouldn't be asking more of your top performers and wear them out. Learn how to engage with those middle folks that want to do amazing work and be a part of something greater than themselves. Also, dear middle folks, silence and not being told something is a poor excuse. If you are unsure or not clear on something ask. If not your supervisor, then a trusted colleague. But, I would ask that you too learn how to engage with your supervisors and leaders. It's not ass-kissing, it's knowing how to so your job proficiently and creating your positive work environment.

Leaders and supervisors, if you're not engaged with your Team Members and unsure how to, start small and keep it simple. Follow these steps:

1. Plan for and schedule team and one-on-one meetings with your direct reports.
2. Be consistent with the meetings and have a planned agenda that allows for all voices to be heard.
3. Get everyone involved in the meetings. Assign roles and responsibilities and rotate those amongst Team Members.
4. Keep meetings relevant and on track. You don't have to use the full time allotted if objectives have been met. Provide direct, purpose and motivation.
5. Keep it positive. Celebrate victories, achievements and milestones, regardless of how big or small.
6. Get feedback. (When you read more about the AAR you'll gain some better skills here.)
7. Follow-up on questions to be answered. It builds trust.

These are just a few examples, as leaders and supervisors you can adjust and build upon them as needed. Also, those Team Members that want to be engaged and have an engaged leadership team, you have to put in the effort. You can do this by:

1. Being present in the meetings. Put the phone on silence, put it out of site and close your laptop (unless you're taking notes).

2. Be prepared to share what you're working on and how others can assist, if needed.
3. Share challenges you've overcome and success stories.
4. Give honest and respectful feedback.
5. Ask for clarification if you do not understand? It's not a sign of weakness, it shows you want to learn and be clear on to perform to the best of your abilities.
6. Put the ego aside and celebrate everyone's successes. Your time will come.
7. If your schedule permits, offer others an opportunity collaborate. We learn from everyone.
8. Follow-up on questions to be answered. It builds trust.

Engagement in the workplace is everyone's responsibility. It's how we succeed as a team and develop an enriching and positive work environment.

"I'm always relieved when someone is delivering a eulogy
and I realize I'm listening to it."
George Carlin

Chapter 5
Leaders are not Listening

I find it quite humorous and annoying when I'm speaking, or anyone else is, and before I can even get to my point or complete the thought I can see the eagerness to speak and give an answer or share an experience begin to form from people's mouth. Before the sentence is even completed they start speaking and attempt to share their two cents. This not only shows they are not listening or wanting to listen, but it's disrespectful. They might have a similar tale or example to share, but they need to stop and wait their turn. Listen first and then provide a response when it's time.

Research from UKG, specializing in HR and workforce management, found that 86% of employees feel colleagues at their organization are not heard fairly or equally – with 47% of teams claiming underrepresented voices are totally undervalued by their leaders (June 2021). Why is this happening? Listening should be an easy skill for the majority of us. Sometimes the easy things to do are the hardest, they are taken for granted and overlooked. Or, in this case not heard or given the opportunity to be heard.

As a young leader when I was still learning and growing I made the mistake of not fully listening to my Team Members. Assuming because I was in-charge I therefore must have the best answers or solutions to any and all questions and challenges that came our way. Wrong. I realized my team stopped providing input, stopped showing up early to start the day and stopped being fully engaged. For a bit I was wondering what had happened, did I miss something, was the team worn out and tired? The answer was yes, yes to all of that.

I failed to deliver fully on my promises to lead. By doing this I created an environment of Team Members not being heard, it was a my way or the highway philosophy. During this time in my life I didn't have a mentor to advise me or be a sound board I could bounce ideas or thoughts off of. I had to do some self-discovery on my own. It began with bringing my team together and asking them what's going on, why the change in attitude and work environment? Once my Team Members realized it was OK to be open and honest the floodgates opened up.

The feedback I received was very clear and to the point. I was demanding. I was a perfectionist. I was just like the others. Suggestions never taken seriously and worse yet, not listening to others' insight and feedback about our team and processes. During this time of discovery for me I did something very important and critical for the moment. I withheld my two cents and any excuses as to why I did what I did or didn't do. I shut my pie hole and simply listened. I watched how each person spoke and the emotions they had. This meeting lasted nearly two hours and it was time well spent. As a young leader I was actually leading by giving my team a voice and finally making them a part of the team.

Looking back, it's kind of funny, during my military days we had so many things to memorize and at the drop of hat be able to recite this or that. One of those items to memorize was our eleven leadership principles, which I did and at every leadership school I went to I was asked to regurgitate them.

Army Leadership Principles (FM 22-100)

1. Know yourself and seek self-improvement.
2. Be technically and tactically proficient.
3. Know your subordinates and look out for their welfare.
4. Keep subordinates informed.
5. Set the example.
6. Insure the task is understood, supervised, and accomplished.
7. Train your subordinates as a team.

8. Make sound and timely decisions.

9. Develop a sense of responsibility among your subordinates.

10. Employ your command in accordance with its capabilities.

11. Seek responsibility and take responsibility for your actions.

In my youthful years they were memorized but not followed fully. Meaning, I didn't include my Team Members properly. The third leadership principal is "Develop a sense of responsibility among your subordinates." For them to have a sense of real responsibility they would have to have bought into me and my processes. But, since I was not effectively listening to them, they were just checking the box.

After our meeting and allowing myself time to take in the feedback and insight I started to make changes, in my leadership style and in truly developing and unifying my team. It began with listening and learning about each of my Team Members. Understanding their background, strengths, weaknesses and what made them tick. I allowed myself to be vulnerable and admit when I didn't know something, asking for my team's opinions and insight.

This took time, nothing happened overnight, but as I stayed the course in my new leadership ways, so did they. Each person grew into their roles and took pride in their work. I provided more opportunities for us to meet as a team and discuss events or concerns. I gave more responsibility to my Team Members, after all I did not have to do everything for it to turn out right. I just had to provide clear direction, purpose and motivation. If something went wrong we discussed why and learned from it, shared with all Team Members so it could be a learning point for all. New ideas and successes were shared as well. Eventually, my team felt comfortable speaking to me about anything and everything.

The most rewarding and best possible insight into how I was leading the right way came when we had to deploy as a team. We worked well together, we each had one another's back and we all came home together as a team. I credit this professional growth and achievement to learning to listen as well as empowering my Team Members to openly speak to me about almost anything. Helping them to feel confident enough to ask me questions about a plan, process or events to come brought our team together.

If you're feeling unheard and you're seeing fellow Team Members go unheard, knowing the leadership is missing out on valuable insight and ideas, then speak up. Speak up in a respectful and professional manner. If you're able to schedule some time to speak with leadership or have that short elevator ride with them, then ask some open-ended questions.

How and who collected the data for the Mark V project?

I was reviewing the data for the Mark V project and would like to share my insight with you.

Could we schedule some time to review the Mark V project? I have some thoughts about it.

Mr. or Misses So-and So, may I ask why you didn't ask the team's feedback or insights?

It may feel uncomfortable to step up and ask these questions or something respectfully similar, but
if not now, when? At some point you must speak-up. Otherwise, it'll continue to eat away at you until one day you explode.

If the targeted small talk fails to work, then email them with the questions and ask for a meeting. You're a valuable part of any team and your experience and insight should be shared and heard.

"Most people do not listen with the intent to understand; they listen with the intent to reply." Stephen R. Covey

Chapter 6
Benefits of Listening

Part of any leadership development program should be learning how to listen, actively listening to what is being said, body language and what is not being said. When I have interviewed for new positions I am quite often asked to share what I believe is a strength of mine. I almost always say listening as one of them.

As Simon Sinek, author of 'Start with Why?' says, "Good listeners have a huge advantage. For one, when they engage in conversation, they make people 'feel' heard. They 'feel' that someone really understands their wants, needs, and desires. And for good reason; a good listener does care to understand." A good listener is worth their weight in gold, especially if they are in a leadership role. A leader that has good listening skills has the potential of guiding their team to new heights.

I truly care about what people are saying and what they are not saying. It helps me to better understand and learn how to assist them and/or lead them. Listening should not be simply thought of as a tool though, it is a valuable resource, one that can give a young leader a big advantage in the workforce.

During one webinar I gave, I shared a graphic about the power of listening. How something so simple, something most of us are capable of and the one thing that can give your team a boost – Listening. Listening is powerful, active listening that is. As a group we discussed twelve benefits that I shared and the participants shared even more.

The Power of Listening (what I shared)
- We learn
- Higher retention rate and advancement
- Better work environment
- Builds trust
- Allows Team Members to be heard
- Helps to understand best course of action
- Transparency
- Helps with open/honest communication
- Develops team dynamics
- Shows respect
- Gets people engaged
- We understand better what is not being said

The power of listening (what participants shared)
- Professional growth
- Better training
- Comradery
- Understanding
- Removes walls and silos
- Rekindles my fire to excel
- Helps with a SWOT (Strength, Weakness, Opportunity, & Threat)
- Establishes a team hierarchy of knowledge
- Saves time and money
- We learn about people's experiences
- Reduces lateness and call offs
- It is mentally healthy

It was surprising to hear everyone chime in on how important it is to listen. I had people saying they have been in their position for several years and not once had their managers or department leads asked for their advice or insight into projects or processes. After the agreed and empathetic murmurs ended, I asked them what ideas they had to help improve processes or ideas for the future within their areas? Once people shared, I recommended them to now share this with their managers and department leads.

If those in-charge won't listen, whether it be due to a busy schedule or assuming all is well because no one is saying otherwise, then the unheard must make themselves heard - doing it politely and respectfully.

When I meet with or speak to a group, whether it's training or conducting an After-Action Review, participants often share with me about how others don't listen and are not asking for opinions and input. I then ask "Have you spoken to them about this and shared your concerns and desire to provide valuable information?" Sadly, the answer I get the majority of the time is "No." Then I am forced to ask "Why not?" This leads to a variety of answers, none of which are worth me typing here.

I remind people that as people, we only know what we know and we don't know what we don't know. That includes what is not being said. Unless someone has that amazing gift of mind reading, otherwise it is tough to know what someone is thinking or wants to share. If a leader is in tune with their office and staff, they may get a feeling that something is up, but let's not put all of our stocks into that option. I'll say it again, the unheard must respectfully and politely make themselves heard if they are not being afforded the opportunity to be listened to.

For those that have a difficult time listening, due to our brains spinning with ideas or the overwhelming desire to add in one's two cents, I have a listening exercise for you.

1. Whatever music genre is your favorite, put it on and listen. Not only to the vocals (if there are any), but take turns listening to each instrument. Focusing on that beat and rhythm it's providing to the song.
2. Visualize how the instrument is being played and its own unique rhythm that it adds.
3. Once the song is over, repeat the process, now focusing on a different instrument.
4. Do this until you have listened to all the instruments that are a part of the song.

I do this from time to time to relax my brain and it helps to turn off my anxiety as well. However, when it comes to listening, it helps to focus and cut through the interfering noise or sounds, the distractions that sometimes prevent us from being good listeners.

I am not saying this will work for everyone, but it has helped me. In fact, research has shown that listening to music can reduce anxiety, blood pressure, and pain as well as improve sleep quality, mood, mental alertness, and memory. It is a total brain workout, per the article "Keep Your Brain Young with Music" (hopkinsmedicine.org).

Hearing is easy, unless you're hard of hearing, listening is the hard part. Actively listening and focusing on what is being said by whomever is speaking takes practice. It takes patience too. Once you're committed to actively listening to what people are saying, you'll hear a lot more of what is going on in the workplace, home, school and in life. Like the old saying goes "Practice makes perfect."

Take your significant other out on a date and if possible, find a cozy place in a corner where you can see all that's happening and you can hear the chatter. Order up some lovely cocktails, perhaps an appetizer or two and begin to listen and watch people. Make sure to share what you're doing with your date and get them involved. My wife and I, as well as our kids, have created long robust stories about people from people watching and listening. Each of us taking turns adding to the tale, according to what we've heard and seen.

Remember this is for fun and to practice your listening skills. If going out isn't your thing, then just be more aware during group and one on one meetings and training sessions to work on actively listening.

"Tell me and I forget, teach me and I may
remember, involve me and I learn."
Benjamin Franklin

Chapter 7
Leading, Learning and Success

Thinking back to my recruiting years with the Army
I remember walking into my new office for the first time
and meeting my fellow recruiters and the supervisor. It was
a very sterile introduction. No smiles, check the block
handshakes, a brief discussion on responsibilities,
expectations, and then shown to my workspace. The only
sign of emotion and life occurred when my supervisor gave
me my assignment, my targeted mission, and the magic
number of people I must recruit each month. The vibes
during this time were of desperation, agitation, and fear.
Boy oh boy did I feel ready and welcomed. I made a joke,
which in my head went over amazingly well, however it

fell upon a stale crowd. Silence and stares filled the room. In the deepest part of my mind I heckled myself.

I remember that day vividly and share that welcoming with groups I speak to and people I train. As I call it today, it was an "Or Else" atmosphere and lack of real leadership. Do this "Or Else!" I am a strong believer that we must learn from the past. Otherwise we'll simply repeat what's not working, must we remind ourselves of the definition of insanity? I think not, even though you are now thinking of it.

It is critical to build upon a team even before a person becomes part of the team. Being open and welcoming sets a standard and if it is a person of interest that you want to hire, it initiates their buy-in process. Once you hire the highly coveted new Team Member, the on-boarding is knocked out, training and continued coaching becomes spotlighted. You have to make these steps just as memorable as the recruiting process. Don't let all the hype turn to blah. During these phases it also allows the supervisor to learn more about the new Team Member and most importantly helps them learn about their strengths and areas of opportunity for the new Team Member.

A new quality Team Member can move the middle. Invigorating the team as well. During these times I often think of Maslow's Hierarchy of needs. Then I put a twist to it and think of how this pertains to people I work with, teams I assist and their work experience. How can I better understand what is needed for them and the team, helping everyone to excel?

As a leader, we must be our team's best cheerleader, advocate for development, and yes, the keeper and enforcer of standards. Over the years I've developed a way for our Team Members to learn more about themselves and to realize the strengths and skills they already possess. The process also allows for leadership to learn as well, and then understand how to better use, train and encourage Team Members. My disclaimer, this will take time. You must be willing to invest the time and be consistent with your team. Otherwise, you are setting them and your work environment up for failure.

During one of my first meetings with a new Team Member I make it a point to learn about who they are. My method involves the discussion of three areas (see figure 1). Personal, Institutional and Professional. Focusing on these three areas allows me to learn not just what's on a resume, but who this person is, what makes them tick, how can I help them to succeed and excel within my team and organization.

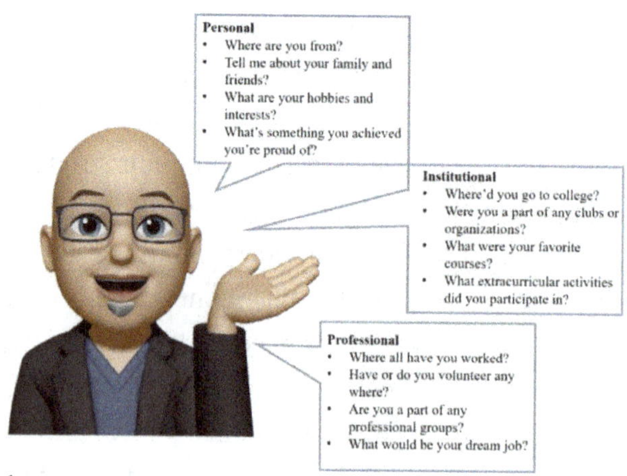

Figure 1

When asking these questions and learning about people I always ask, at the end of each area, "What are your future plans and goals?" I want to know if they have a personal goal of running a marathon. If they plan to go back to school. Or, if they see themselves running their own company someday. My goal as a leader is to help them on their journey. I can't help them train for a marathon, but I can ensure we have a work-life balance in our office, so they have time to train. As leaders, supervisors and fellow colleagues, are we asking ourselves these questions:

- What are we learning about our Team Members to have a quality and trustful work relationship?
- Are we using our Team Members to the best of their abilities?
- Do our Team Members have and know a path to growth and success?

This is a two-way street though. Most people will only want to focus on hard factual evidence as to why they are qualified, capable, and even worth an employer's time. We don't give ourselves credit for the tangible life experiences we've had that can correlate and assist us in our job searches, resume writing and when working. This is not about stretching the truth, this is about sharing the truth. Taking credit for all you've achieved thus far in your life, diving deeper than the earned diploma or two years spent at Dairy Queen.

I remind you to not overstep any human resource boundaries. If you're unsure of an interview question or how best to engage with a Team Member, ask your HR representative, research and learn.

I had a young recruiter that worked for me and he was very polite, sharp looking and had a great sense of humor. But he could not talk to people he didn't already know, it was hard for him to strike up a conversation. A bit shy and lacking some confidence. My first thought was "why are you in this business?" Fortunately, I had taken the time to learn about him, using the three mentioned categories as my base. I realized there was a disconnect on both of our parts. I wasn't placing him in an opportunity to excel and he didn't understand how to use all of his acquired talents. As I have said, this takes time, trial and error. I took the extra time to develop a plan for him. By simply assisting him in realizing he had the skills, making him aware that he's been using them for a better part of his life, and letting him know I believed in him, he was then able to better understand how to and what he needed to do to succeed.

Some trial and error still took place, but they became lessons learned. They also became less frequent as he progressed. With each month and quarter that passed I slowly added on more responsibility, until he was fully up and running. He had all the needed tools, knew what resources were available and how to use them and he knew the "why" behind assigned tasks and missions. He became a contributing member of our team.

This process was not popular with my senior leadership. They had a "now" mentality. "He's been to the Recruiting and Retention School, he graduated, he should be ready. No excuses!" Is what I was often told. Respectfully, I disagreed and did my best to explain my process and what was needed beyond the learning that took place in school. It was not always popular but needed and it paid off. My young soldier found his groove. He wasn't always successful, but he learned to learn from those mistakes and failures.

Regardless of the leadership role you find yourself in, there is always time to lead. Part of leading is learning about our team, people we associate with and even ourselves. You may have heard of how a leader should never ask you to do something they have not done or would not do themselves. I believe leaders need to take it a step further and add that they too should never ask you to do something that they cannot still do.

As an example, during my military recruiting days I would often challenge my recruiters. We would target a certain area to blitz, meaning all hands-on deck to recruit in this area. A combination of phone calls, face to face canvassing and basically talking to anyone and everyone that would listen to us. Part of the challenge was that I would also participate, each of us had established plans and goals. Whoever got the most leads, appointments and first to put someone from that blitz into the Army won. It was important that I not only talked the talk, but walked the walk. Not to brag, but most of the time I won. When it came time to put the person or people in the Army I would assign them to a recruiter that was doing well and handling business, a kind of reward, a thank you for all you do.

I had experience on my side. The experience of winning and losing, hearing all kinds of rejections and learning how to overcome them. Understanding who the decision maker was and most importantly if the person was even qualified. My team was able to see me in action and learn in real time. This not only helped them to excel, but helped me to better communicate with them. They learned I was not full of BS and what I trained them on and continuously discussed with them worked.

Dear colleagues and fellow Team Members, if your leadership and supervisors are not asking you some of these questions. Or, learning how best to help you excel within the organization you're a part of. Then you need to be your own best cheerleader and ask them how and what you can do to grow professionally within your role. I caution you, do not ask questions you are not ready to hear the answer to. If you are truly ready for professional growth, then understand that even negative feedback can be productive. Provided you learn and research how best to overcome those challenges. Easy questions such as:

- What are some opportunities for me to grow and learn in my position?
- What do you see as my weaknesses?
- Are there any projects coming up that I can be a part of to help me grow within the organization?
- What would be the next step for me to take professionally within the organization?
- What training, courses and/or certifications should I look into, that would help me advance within the organization?

If you are meet with "I'm not sure." or "Let me think about it." Then respectfully ask to schedule some time to go over this information.

Too many organizations list "Growth opportunities," "Professional develop provided," and "We coach and mentor our Team Members." In their job descriptions. Designed to get the potential applicant excited to apply. Then you get hired, start work and a year later the only training you've received are mandatory online classes covering Information Security Awareness, HIPAA Compliance and Workplace Violence. All of these are important, but have they helped you to take the next steps in your career?

If you find yourself in a situation like this and you are generally happy with your position and organization, then it's time for you to be your own best cheerleader and inquire about opportunities. Also, if a leadership or management role is something you don't want to explore and take on, that is OK too. It's important you know your professional wants and needs. You should never be chastised for not wanting to lead. It's not for everyone and once again, that is OK.

"Loyalty to petrified opinion never yet broke a chain or freed a human soul." Mark Twain

Chapter 8
Be Loyal to Yourself First

You know what? You just might be doing all or some of the things I've discussed on your own or with management and leadership and you find yourself repeating information like a skipping record and they never seem to get it. Or, you realize they are not listening and their actions or lack of them show they do not want to. Well, at least you've tried. It might be time to explore other career options.

For a little over a year I worked with a wonderful restaurant company as their recruiting manager. I loved their mission and sustainability mantra. My immediate boss was one of the best people I've worked with. She allowed me to do what I do best and inspired me with her actions and work. However, I was having a constant challenge of getting restaurant general managers to follow and act upon the recruiting process guidelines I had developed and implemented. Some tried and some simply didn't. I made the process as easy and as least time consuming as possible.

To better understand this, you should know how the management hierarchy was in each restaurant. You had the General Manager (GM), who was responsible for the overall success or failure of the restaurant. Then you have the Front of the House management team and the Back of the House management team. Front of the House had two assistant managers, as did the GM. They oversaw waiters and waitresses, hosts, bartenders, and bussers/runners. Back of the House had the Chef and two sous-chefs. They took care of the kitchen staff, line-cooks, prep-cooks, and dishwashers. Working together they make a restaurant flow.

I gave a presentation about the recruiting process I developed and was implementing during a quarterly GM meeting, sent out bi-monthly reminders and data sheets about prospects and applicants. I called, emailed and took time to go to the restaurants to assist. I even pre-screened many of the applicants to save the restaurant management time. When emailing I always cc'd my supervisor, the regional GM and the COO. I never got follow up emails from the regional GM or COO and rarely from the GMs. It remained a challenge and at this point it was starting to hurt my head.

I had spent a week in one of our major restaurants that was having personnel and recruiting troubles. Knowing the GM's talk often amongst one another, I wanted to prove that if they were to follow guidelines and recruiting philosophy they would achieve better restaurant results. By hiring quality over just a pulse, providing training and holding everyone accountable on an equal playing field, then you could assemble a great team. Which would lead to better service, higher guest reviews and achieve that dollar bottom line and then some.

Well, to cut to the chase it worked. I got the restaurant better Team Members, some people were let go and we helped the GM learn to listen, engage, train and hold people accountable. Word did get around to the other GMs, but some still didn't follow guidance and kept asking for more people, more leads. I spoke with my supervisor about it and she listened, offered advice and most importantly she validated what I was doing was right and to keep at it.

I kept at it for over a year. Even adjusting to meet the needs of some restaurant management teams. My goal and the strategy I was attempting to implement looked like this:

1. Post the request position within 24 hours (my responsibility)
2. Contact new applicants within 24 hours (now it's the restaurant's time)
3. Conduct in-person interviews within 48 hours of initial phone screening

4. Follow-up with candidates within 24 hours of interview (if not hired on the spot)
5. If hired, schedule on-boarding within 72 hours (unless waiting on job notice)
6. Prior to on-boarding assign a mentor, schedule training days
7. Day 1 of employment complete all necessary hire paperwork and send to HR
8. Introduce to mentor/trainer, start learning the business

I believed if we could follow this process we would attract and hire better talent and improve our retention as well. This was about having good communication and respect for one's time. Setting the standard and being accountable.

During my initial training with the GM's I even gave them a recruiting handbook, specifically designed for their restaurant and area. I can honestly say without hesitation I did my best to communicate, follow-up and engage with the restaurant teams and our corporate Team Members.

In the fall of 2019, we had our corporate retreat, where we discussed the past year and planned out our KPIs (key performance indicators) and shared ideas for the new year to come. When it was my turn to share I presented some data about what I had achieved during the year and challenges faced. I shared my recruiting methodology and process to the team, something I had done at least a dozen times. I wanted everyone to know about it and share it.

Before transitioning to my next slide our COO spoke up and said "I have never seen this. I swear to God this is something I have never seen. How do the GMs know this?" Initially I actually thought he was joking, but he wasn't and I was at a loss for words. No one in the meeting spoke up about how I've shared it quite often, trained people on it to include the COO and the people in that room just stared at me. Waiting for my answer. "This is something I have shared multiple times with management" I replied. I didn't want to be confrontational, lord knows it was tough to not use my super power of sarcasm.

I completed my presentation and was still shocked over what I had heard. I knew at that moment when I was sitting back in my seat that it was time for me to find a new opportunity. Nothing I was going to do was going to sink in. Leadership didn't buy into it and from my perspective didn't give it the time of day. It was not a priority for them, though they often spoke about finding top quality candidates, hiring talented people and training GMs, it was a mix of lip service and not a priority for them. The EBITDA was their main focus (an accounting acronym that stands for Earnings Before Interest, Taxes, Depression, and Amortization. It is a metric used to determine a restaurant's worth before adding factors like depression, taxes, and interest.). A month and half later I accepted a position with the Fairmont and respectfully resigned.

Be loyal to yourself first and foremost. If you're giving it your all and doing your best to get things done, communicating with non-responsive leaders and you feel you're just spinning in circles, then it's time to search for greener pastures. It's OK to quit bad jobs, managers and supervisors. I fully understand that most of us need to work and make a living. But, how much is your mental health worth? Never let it get to a point where you explode and paint a bad memory of yourself in other's minds.

As much time as working consumes our lives, we deserve to ensure it's worth our time and efforts. I have no hard feelings or resentments towards that COO and the rest of the team. My style wasn't right for them and vise-versa. I am still in contact with many or my old Team Members from there and have some nice memories and experiences. It can be tough making those hard decisions. That's part of adulting and being an adult at times can suck.

"The only thing worse than training your employees and having them leave is not training them and having them stay." Henry Ford

Chapter 9
Train Them and They'll Lead

Our managers, supervisors and leaders need training. The old and the young. Too many are in roles that require leading others and many do not know how. They may know the job skills and duties down to a tee. However, when it comes to interacting and actually leading and training a team, they may not be proficient. While 83% of organizations believe it's important to develop leaders at every level of the company, only 5% of businesses have implemented leadership development at all levels. That is a stat I found on Zippia.com (Sept. 2022). Why such a low number? Unfortunately, the idea tends to get pushed off to the side. Some due to budget, others due to time and some is good old-fashioned lip service. "Look at us, we're discussing leadership and improving our leaders." "The board will love that."

Leadership development does require time. The time to check out a book from the library and read it. Or, buy one on Amazon and having it delivered the next day. Perhaps swing by a book store and pick one up, a perk is that book stores smell good too. Get crazy and login to LinkedIn and take a free one-hour class on leadership development.

Stay with me now, I'm about to get totally absurd, make time on your work calendar, let's say thirty minutes, and do some professional self-development. Read the book you acquired or a quick class online. It really is that simple. The hard part is planning and doing it. The even harder part is to not overthink it and implement some of the lessons learned and training little by little. No need to do a complete 180, just take it in steps, one by one.

Do not let time and the lack of it prevent you from training and learning. I could easily go off on a tangent about time management, but that's a whole other topic and write up. I will add though, that effective and efficient managers, supervisors and leaders know how to manage their time. That too can be trained and learned.

I have some good and not so good memories of my time in the Army. One thing I do appreciate from all of my years of service was the focus on leadership development. As you progress in the Army and achieve more rank you'll also be required to attend a certain level of leadership courses. Beyond basic training and your advanced individual training, it starts with the Primary Leadership Develop Course, that changed to the Warrior Leader Course and now it is the Basic Leader Course. This month-long course introduces beginner level leadership ideas, philosophies and characteristics of how a leader should lead.

Stick around for a bit longer in the Army and achieve more rank you eventually need to attend the Advanced Leader Course, then the Senior Leader Course, the First Sergeant Academy, on to the U.S. Army Sergeants Major Academy and if lucky enough you get to attend the Command Sergeants Major Academy. All that is just on the enlisted side of the house in the Army. The officers have a whole bunch of training opportunities as well.

As soldiers progress in the military, leadership training and development is mandatory. This does not mean that each person who graduates from any of those courses will be a good leader. All the traits and skills come together to make a good leader. But for most, the lessons learned help them to better lead their teams.

So why can't corporate America and business do the same things? Not as in depth, but something to help develop people. We cannot simply add some LinkedIn Learning links to a web page and assume people will take the time watch and learn. Help a promising manager become a good leader. Turn a supervisor into a mentor and prepare young leaders for bigger responsibilities. Take the time to set people up for success. If they are not ready then do not rush it or attempt to find a warm body to fill the role.

This will only lead to more trouble and poor productivity by the Team Members.

When it comes to this subject and our Team Members I have a simple saying that I share, "Train and retain." A sign of this should hang in every leaders and supervisor's office as a reminder (see figure 2).

Figure 2

If we commit to training our Team Members and live up to all the benefit mumbo-jumbo we put in job postings we will retain our top talent. Fact.

SHRM's 2022 research report on Workplace Learning and Development Trends discovered that 48% of employees agree that training opportunities were a factor in choosing a company. While 76% said they are more likely to stay with a company that offers continuous training. Want to know how to assist your human resource department and recruiters, and train your team? Provide real professional training opportunities that help them to develop and grow. Then you can reap the rewards.

Listen to your team and learn what kind of training they want and need. What will inspire and motivate them? Make sure to learn about and review the trainer and material. Is the information or context out of date? Is the trainer boring? This is important. One of the biggest complaints I hear from Team Members is that the material was dull and dated, death by power point and the trainer wasn't engaging. What a waste of time and money. If we do our research though, we can prevent such things from happening.

Look within your organization. Who is doing and trying new things, something exciting that is relevant to the work environment? Find these energetic people and have them speak with your team and provide them with some interesting and inspiring training. It most likely is free and you'll only need to coordinate the time and place.

Perhaps challenge your Team Members by assigning them a training to give to the team. This also gets people engaged. By giving them some simple guidance on subject and expectation, then let them run with it. Have fun with it, make it interactive and memorable.

According to Udemy (2018), nearly half of employees said they've quit a job because of a bad manager. What's more, 56% think managers are promoted prematurely and 60% think managers need more managerial training. We owe it to our managers, supervisors and leaders to prepare them for the responsibility of leading our greatest asset, our people. We owe it to our people to have quality leaders in place.

"Many ideas grow better when transplanted into another mind than the one where they sprang up."
Oliver Wendell Holmes

Chapter 10
The Filtration System

Every organization I have worked for and assisted shares what a dynamic and wonderful culture the company has. Once the internet was developed and streamlined to what it is today, you'll now see Instagram stories of Team Members with big smiles, web pages with images of a variety of ethnicities and it's always a focus, our culture, with the leadership. Doesn't it suck though when you join such a company and discover the façade? People are working in silos, communication is filtered and smiles are as rare as Astatine.

The key word I want to focus on is "filtered." Having sat in board meetings and senior leadership meetings I've heard some great ideas and detailed plans on how to achieve wonderful things. Then as the information is dispersed it becomes filtered and before you know it the information becomes a one liner to lower level staff. "Complete this report and have it back to me by Thursday before noon." That's all the information they get. Not knowing anything beyond completing the report, get it to the boss by Thursday before noon.

Funny enough managers, supervisors and leaders think they are saving time by leaving out all the juicy meat and potatoes. When in reality they are creating more work with an unclear why. Leaving Team Members thinking "As if I don't already have enough to do." So other work gets pushed aside and those waiting on that stuff get to wait a little longer. With no reason as to why, schedules get manipulated to adjust for the extra work to complete in the short period of time.

What if we just shared the "why," if not the entire plan? A great majority of people work for an organization because their values align or they believe in what the company is doing and its mission. So why are managers and leaders not sharing everything taking place, appropriate need to know info, in the organization? If part of your values and mission is to be transparent and to build a successful team then you might want to share more with your Team Members.

The pandemic turned almost everyone's world into a spinning crazy blur, employees have had plenty of time to contemplate. Some of that contemplation has been about work. In a January 2022 article on Gartner.com titled "Employees Seek Personal Value and Purpose at Work. Be Prepared to Deliver." 52% of employees surveyed said the pandemic made them question their day-to-day job. 50% say the pandemic changed their expectations towards their employer. Very interesting. With this knowledge we should be ensuring we are making the work environment a better one. This includes informing our Team Members on the day-to-day plans and goals of the organization.

Having a Team Member feel included and part of a team within an organization is powerful. A Team Member that feels included and valued will stay with an organization longer. The work relationships they establish and the collaborative environment they are a part of becomes a valuable benefit. One that money cannot buy. One of the big reasons for the "Great Resignation" during and after the COVID-19 pandemic was that this newly allotted time gave many people time to think about what is truly important to them and this included the workplace.

There are plenty of statistics on this, but let's not get wrapped up on them, they are what you make of them. The ones I have shared are a snapshot of perhaps a few thousand people's perspectives. However, when similar polls or surveys are completed all over the place by all kinds of organizations and the results are saying the same things, then we should listen and learn.

An informed Team Member is an engaged Team Member. If they aren't engaged after you've shared all the plans and road map forward, then perhaps it's time for you to help them update their resume and explore other opportunities. I hear the Department of Motor Vehicles is always hiring unengaging people.

Information is valuable, I can understand why some want to keep it all to themselves - if we're talking about national security or trade secrets. Otherwise share the details and the full plan, or plan up to this point with your Team Members and challenge them to succeed and go beyond expectations.

There is a good time and wrong time to share information, depending on its nature and people in attendance that need to hear it. However, don't always wait for the perfect time or ensure that everyone is present to hear this wonderful plan or news. Time can make information irrelevant or dated.

I ask groups sometimes if they'd rather move forward with a plan that is a solid 80% worked out or have 100% of a plan completed and possibly miss the boat? Most agree on the 80%, some ask if there will be another boat. There is always another boat, but not for the same opportunity perhaps. It's OK to take risks and discover as we move forward.

One of my last After-Action Reviews (AAR) I conducted during my military service was for a battalion training operation, simulated training like a war game. Prior to the AAR I had reviewed the operation order with the battalion commander, watched the training unfold and observed bits and pieces of his team in action. Once the training was over, everyone and all things were accounted for. We met at a small theater to conduct the formal AAR. I met with leadership first and got their two cents. "The training could not have gone any better," "It went exactly as planned," "Our teams knew their job and executed it precisely," "This will be a quick AAR." This is the initial feedback leadership shared with me.

I then reminded them of the AAR process and that this is a learning opportunity, they'll hear a variety of perspectives and it's OK to disagree respectfully. Everyone agreed and we moved into the theater.

When speaking to the group, in this case about two hundred soldiers, larger than normal, but the commander wanted all of his units that participated in this training event to be together for this AAR, I share the ground rules. I want your perspective, speak for yourself not others. Be respectful and listen to others. It's OK to disagree and have a productive open and honest discussion. Most importantly, during this meeting there is no rank or time in service trump card, meaning we all equal and have a voice.

Like all other AAR's I've facilitated I begin with asking "what was supposed to happen?" and like many AAR's you initially get complete silence. No one wants to go first and I've asked key leadership to not chime in at this point. So, like most AARs I smile and stare around the room looking for just the right person to call upon. Searching for the lowest ranking person. Eyes briefly meet mine and quickly turn away, heads slowly turn down and some even attempt to melt towards the floor. It's quite humorous.

Then I see the person I want to call upon. A new private, no rank on his collar and still has the signs of a basic training haircut. He's not looking at me and I can see from his body language he's making wishes to Santa, the first star of the night and a shooting star begging to not be called upon. So, I move closer, read his name tag and call upon him.

"Private Smith (not his name, must protect the wishers of the world), from your perspective what was supposed to happen?" Silence fills the room, he slowly looks up as if asking "who me?" Then a voice is heard, "I'm not sure, can't remember." Such a poor excuse, as if I was going to accept it and move on to someone else, silly wisher. "Come on now, don't be shy, what did you know about this event and the plan?" I ask in a gentler tone, reminding him it's OK to share your two cents. No one is going to be getting in trouble for sharing their perspective today, provided it's done respectfully.

"Sergeant, all I knew…" a pause in his answer and a crackle in his voice… "all I knew was to get on a helicopter at 0500 and we'd be dropped off at a certain grid coordinate." His voice got quieter as he finished his sentence and he had started to melt again into his seat.

I repeated what he said and ask him "This is all you were aware of?" "Yes, and we were dropped off at the wrong grid coordinates." Was his reply and it seemed to take all he had to get those words out. I repeated once again what he had just shared, with a slight giggle, I've been there. He then added that his team's supplies were dropped off at the right grid coordinates and he and his team chief had to figure out where they were. When attempting to reach their immediate supervisor over the radio, they realized they also had the wrong radio frequency and security information.

This young soldier's team chief confirmed the events and had a bit more knowledge about what was to take place, but not the full plan or the whys behind it. This team spent the majority of the training exercise trying to find and communicate with leadership. Thankfully this was only training.

Point of the story? Never assume everyone knows the plan or that lower leadership and managers are providing a clear picture of it and events that will be taking place or needed actions. This isn't about micromanaging others, but validating that all members of your team know the "why" and the purpose for it is clear and precise.

I spoke with the battalion commander after the AAR and we discussed the feedback. He was disappointed how his multi-paged operation order had been filtered so much according to each team's responsibility and the big picture wasn't clearer. His senior leadership and junior officers knew the info pretty well, but everyone needs to know it. In training you provide info in a step-by-step method, but in real combat that is not an option. Teams need the full information and with that information and the appropriate training received, success can be achieved.

The same is true in workplaces around the world. Team Members want to know and should be made aware of the big picture and how they can help to achieve it. This is why the word "Teamwork" was created.

I feel bad for Team Members when I am facilitating an AAR and I ask "What did you know of the plan and process that was to take place?" I can see that they don't want to offend or bust anyone out. The wheels are rapidly spinning inside their heads, thinking of what to say that won't come across as rude or irresponsible. Too often the answers I receive are very much in line with what that young private said. "All I knew…"

Just as leadership and supervisors need to fully inform their Team Members, we too as Team Members need to seek additional information and/or knowledge. People like knowing that what they are doing, or will be doing, has an impact on other plans and initiatives. When we know the big picture, we tend to put forth a better product.

Leaders and supervisors, if you are not providing direction, purpose and motivation to your Team Members, then I ask why not? You don't have to bring out the pom-poms and cheer, just share the "Why." Providing clarity, timelines and deadlines, how this piece of the puzzle fits into the picture and its importance shouldn't be considered extra information. If you're working in some top-secret organization and there are clearance requirements, then OK, I get it. If not, share. Sharing builds trust.

As a Team Member, here are a few questions you can ask, ones to better help you understand if you're not being given clearly defined expectations on a task or assignment:

- When is this due and to whom?
- Is this a part of a bigger project? If so, who is the project lead?
- Is there anything in particular you're needing or hoping to discover from this assignment?
- May we schedule a check-in, to go over my initial work and/or findings?
- Will anyone else be working on this besides me?

These are important questions, because they allow you to connect the dots and discover the who, what, when, why and if needed the how. Asking open ended clarifying questions should not be thought of as a weakness or coming across as not confident. In fact, it shows confidence and that you, as a vital Team Member, want to do and share exceptional work.

"If you have passion, there is no need for excuses because your enthusiasm will trump any negative reasoning you might come up with. Enthusiasm makes excuses a nonissue."
Wayne Dyer

Chapter 11
Going from Mundane to Enthusiastic

Just as leaders, supervisors and managers should share the full details of a plan or objectives for the year, Team Members should be asking for them. One should never complain about not knowing what's going on if they have never asked what's going on. That's like blaming the spoon and fork for making you a little thicker than you'd like.

We have a level of responsibility to ask questions, to understand the why behind things and how you and your

Team Members' roles and actions fit into this puzzle. If you are not getting answers then ask someone else and respectfully make leadership and those in supervisor or managerial positions do their jobs.

I feel more engaged and purpose driven when I know what's going on and how I am a part of it. From speaking with fellow Team Members and years of research I am confident in saying that most others feel this way too.

Often, I read and hear about people's dissatisfaction with their current employment situation. Some complain about co-workers, the hours, the commute, the pay and whatever else triggered their annoyance alarm. If I am speaking with someone or listening to a conversation I enjoy asking follow-up questions. What is it about your co-workers that you dislike? What kind of work schedule would you like to establish with your supervisor? Mostly, because I am curious and I like learning what others do. Plus, I do enjoy helping others, if possible, and if they are willing to listen.

What never ceases to amaze me is that when I ask those questions I get piss-poor answers. Such as "No." and nothing else. Or, "Not yet, but I'm thinking about it." "My manager is always busy and doesn't have the time." If those are reasons you're willing to accept, then you should be willing to accept a crummy work life. Failure to never take-action or taking action too late equals a crummy work life.

I know there are some semi legitimate excuses, and I say semi because an excuse is only good for a short period of time. Meetings end. Vacations end and people return to work. The stars can and do align to have those conversations with supervisors or Team Members. The hard part for many is simply doing it. Sharing concerns, asking why about something, expressing one's dislikes or what obstacles can be a challenge. After all, you don't want to come across as someone that's complaining, a pest or cry baby.

This is where our lovely word "respect" comes into play. Take the time to write down your concerns, dislikes and lack of understanding. Formulate them into respectful questions that show you want to learn, understand and improve the working environment. When we are respectful in our delivery of information it tends to be well received. If you're presenting a problem, have a solution to follow it up with factual supporting information. Be like the mob, make them an offer they can't refuse. Without the violence though. Be prepared for counter offers and/or deeper questions about the situation. You have to do your homework and be ready.

This is a great opportunity to reflect on your actions or lack of action. What have you actually done to improve your situation or the work environment? Did it work? If not, why? Did part of the plan work, but fell apart in the end? Why? Before we can go pointing fingers we must have a clear understanding of what we have done, have not done, the mistakes made, the lessons learned, who we've included in the process and how that went. It's part of your homework, or should we call it work-work? Since it is work being done at work, unless you're in school, do your best to not take work home.

I do a lot of brainstorming, for the most part of it I'm alone. Marker in hand in front of my dry erase board, talking to myself, jotting down thoughts as jazz plays in the background. Then taking a break and coming back to it and fine tuning my ideas or process. I like getting it out and having that visual image to look upon and ponder. Sometimes, I'll ask a colleague to come participate, even if they are not part of the process, just to get a new perspective and insight.

It could be over an event that just ended and I'm getting all my thoughts out or it could be a forthcoming event that I am preparing for. I do the same for goals in life and things I want to do at work. It helps me to understand my why and see all the different roads I can take or not take. If you haven't guessed by now, the why, is pretty darn important. Everyone should be used to it. Why this? Why that? A classic we have all most likely answered and some have asked, "Why do you want to work for…?" Knowing the why helps us to become active and contributing Team Members.

Just as a good leader should provide their Team Members with direction, purpose and motivation, so must the individual establish this for themselves. What direction do you want to go in life? Become CEO? Open your own business? Be a happy and contributing Team Member? Then you should ask yourself and understand what is your purpose? What do I want to achieve in life and in work? What or who do I want to have an impact on? Finally, what is your motivation? Is it to retire early and chill on the beach and watch every sunrise or sunset that remains? Maybe it's to work long enough and earn enough to get your kids through college.

You owe it to yourself to have a clear picture of

what you want out of life. Whether it be the work force or private life. Write your goals and dreams down, put them in a place so you see them multiple times a day and then take at least one step forward each day to achieve them. I know, I know, you've heard that a million times, blah, blah, blah. It becomes white noise. I get it. But when you accept that, then you've accepted to simply be a collection of atoms that is taking up space and please stop complaining about things you won't do a damn thing about. Harsh? Yup, but it's the truth, otherwise prove me and everyone else, including yourself wrong.

If you are actively asking why and taking the time to listen and understand then rock on with your bad self. But, it can get tough on this journey. You might have to ask yourself "Why am I still working here?" If what you are doing or trying to do isn't being heard or given an opportunity. You've given it your all, you've asked and asked, shared and shared and have gone through more dry erase markers than budget allows. Well then, perhaps it's time to explore other opportunities that align with your goals and ideas?

Team Members that started as engaged Team Members can unfortunately become unengaged due to the hierarchy not listening and not acting. Some will sadly accept it and become paycheck collectors. Is that wrong? Hard to say. I think it's wrong if you let the lack of action by others kill your aspirations. If that is happening you must explore other opportunities ASAP!

I have yet to meet or read about anyone that enjoys job hunting. But you owe it to yourself to be happy in your work life. So maybe you are a paycheck collector for a while until you find a new and better opportunity. But please, please, please don't stop trying to improve what is going on in the place you're currently at. When it's time, you can walk away saying with 100% clarity that you tried and did your best.

Being an engaged Team Member is not about kissing ass or agreeing with everything a supervisor or senior leader says or does. Being an engaged Team Member is about taking the time to see how things are from your perspective, from the role you're in and how things can be improved. Sharing your insight and experience with others on how things can be improved or changed to increase team efficiency and effectiveness.

It's taking the time to help train new colleagues, helping a colleague that is struggling (not doing their work, but helping them prioritize and manage their work day). We are not going to be on our A game every day, it just does not happen. On those days we are doing our best to be productive and make the day count. Being an engaged Team Member is doing your work to the best of your ability and discovering how you can improve upon your skills and daily responsibilities.

As an engaged Team Member, you ask clarifying questions, you ask about the unknown, so you can have a clear picture of what's going on in your team, in your department and in the company. No one wants to show up for work one day and see that the doors are locked and the company has closed up shop overnight, like Enron did in the early 2000's.

An engaged Team Member respectfully holds leadership accountable, just as they would hold their Team Members accountable. It's a two-way street my friend.

"Understanding your employee's perspective can go a long way towards increasing productivity and happiness."
Kathryn Minshew

Chapter 12
Everyone is Invited

Dear Janitorial Service Department, Housekeeping, Security, Interns, Temporary Hires, Soon to Retire, Newbies, everyone involved, you are cordially invited to participate in this meeting about this and a little about that, then we'll discuss something about here and there.

When we have a meeting to discuss events or projects that took place we sometimes, well, a lot of the time, fail to invite all parties involved in the process. As if one segment of the participants involved can produce a clear picture about the event. They might be able to establish what things took place or didn't from their perspective, but a clear overall idea will never be achieved unless everyone is invited to share their perspective about the event or project.

In one of my first After-Action Reviews with a university I was scheduled to facilitate, I asked the organizer for all planning material, project scope, timeline matrix and anything they could provide to me, so I could have a solid understanding about what was supposed to happen and the process. I also asked what other departments and participants would be joining us. "It's just my department" was the reply I received. I then asked a follow-up question. "Did this project only involve members of your department?" The supervisor looked at me as if I was stupid and said "No, of course not. But, this is just for our department's learning."

I appreciated that he used the word learning, it showed he kind of understood the process. But, to fully learn from any event or project that took place or is taking place, we have to have all available perspectives. His department would not know about how the project was perceived and dealt with from members of Human Resources or IT. They would only have their perspective from the dealings they had and they just might think it went as smooth as glass. Not knowing what HR and IT had to do to help them. How they had to adjust their own projects and plans, determine who would help them and when.

The supervisor and I discussed this and I shared why it's important to invite and include all people that were actively engaged with this project. Regardless, if they only had to forward a few emails or they were the project lead. We all have our own perspective of what took place, why things were completed like they were and all the how's, where's and when's. This is why it is important to include all voices in the discussion.

Sometimes the stars may not align to have all perspectives present. Then, it is important to at least have a representative from each area, department, team, and organization present. In a situation like this, as the facilitator, I simply ask if they had an AAR with Team Members that assisted in the project, collected their feedback and insight so it can be shared with everyone during the formal AAR. I will also send out an anonymous AAR survey to all participants and then share the feedback during the actual AAR.

For us to properly put the puzzle together we have to first have all the pieces available. Sure, we can identify areas we excelled in and areas we dropped the ball within our team, but then we need to know how this affected other teams and vice versa. When we come together as a whole we can respectfully share our perspectives, of the good, the bad and the ugly.

I always share some ground rules prior to facilitating an AAR and the first one is that this AAR is a respectful discussion and it's OK to disagree. We may not agree on how things should have gone and the why behind them, but an AAR is an opportunity to learn and discover all the whys, from all levels and perspectives. As the facilitator it is important to keep the process flowing and ensuring communication is respectful. During the process I may act more like a mediator and help two parties find common ground or an agreed upon process/next steps.

You may have heard the saying "None of us are in this alone" though at times things can seem overwhelming and you're about to pull out your hair. Or, after hours of research you just can't find the answer on your own, your eyes are bulging and your head is about to explode. Ask for assistance, get someone else's two cents and let's learn together.

One of the biggest issues I see in organizations is that departments work in silos and rarely reach out to other departments for assistance or ask if they've dealt with something similar. Then they end up repeating the same processes that just failed them three times prior. A sad waste of time and people power.

When we include all pieces of the puzzle into an AAR we discover that we're not the only one's dealing with a similar concern or issue. We learn how other departments or teams overcame the hurdle and managed to move forward. By having as many participants that helped out with the project or event, regardless of duration or roles, we get the opportunity to hear and listen to multiple perspectives. The insight is so valuable and it can assist us to make the needed improvements. We can take these lessons learned and those by others, to help our team to improve and potentially not repeat the what not to do and mitigate as much risk as possible.

In chapter 17 you'll learn much more about planning for and having an AAR. During the planning phase, which should take place at the same time you are planning your event, you take time to identify parties involved and invite them to the formal AAR. Think about all the people and departments you had to work with to make your event happen. Such as:

- Security
- Janitorial
- IT
- Accounting & Contracts
- Catering
- Participants of the event

These groups are sometimes left out of the AAR process, leaving assumptions to take their place. For an event or project to be successful every party involved has to do their job/role properly. Don't take for granted that anyone or any department will do their job to the precise detail you need them to. You must respectfully communicate and allow them to share. Not to be too cheesy, but teamwork makes the dream work.

"If one is lucky, a solitary fantasy can totally transform one million realities." Maya Angelou

Chapter 13
A Shared Vision

Thinking of some of the statistics on why people apply to or pick an organization to become a part of and what people are looking for in a company, especially post pandemic, it's not surprising that so many job seekers and actively employed lookers want and need that significant connection with an organization. A shared connection of values and beliefs, plus having a shared vision of what is possible to achieve and aim for in the future are important as well. Where are we headed as a team? A clearly defined and understood roadmap going forward is important for

Team Members. It helps to give them a purpose and to buy into what the company is doing.

This blueprint is the guide, the answer, and the reminder. When unsure about a process or event, one should be able to look back at the roadmap and shared vision to help guide them. Does this event fall in line with our team and organizational vision, values, and roadmap? If not, why? Should we be doing it? If yes, then why? What is the connection? You can even go as far as asking yourself at the end of the day "Did I take a positive step forward in achieving strategic steps on our roadmap?" If not, why? If yes, then "what can I do tomorrow to build upon it?"

These are quick check-ins with yourself and the team. If you're in a leadership position you should be doing this quite often. Ensuring the vehicle is pointed in the right direction and moving forward. If it's not, guess what? Ask why. Keep your Team Members engaged in the process, not only making sure they do what is needed, but that they too are sharing insight and perspectives.

Want to decrease turnover in your organization? Then don't just share your vision, but have a shared vision with your team and new hires. Hire for the right fit, not just a beating heart that can move paper or send emails from one person to another.

Want to increase morale in your organization? Then don't just share your vision, have a shared vision with your team and new hires. Do weekly check-ins with the team and listen to them on how things are going and why.

Want to increase overall performance in the workplace? Guess what? Yup, then don't just share your vision, have a shared vision with your team and new hires. Having a united vision equals a strong purpose and leads to higher productivity in Team Members.

None of this is revolutionary or brand new, coming out of my fingertips like magic on this computer I'm typing on. It's known stuff. It's just that some can't see the forest through the trees. They do not actively listen. They do not speak up about concerns. They have stopped being engaged. Some have found it easier to remain silent and just do what they have to do, you know, collect that paycheck and move on.

As a leader, I know things do not change overnight. Getting everyone on the same page is work. Especially if you're in an organization that loves to introduce new things that last for only a month or so. Then something new comes along. Your boss read the back cover of a new business book and can't wait to try out the concept in their office. That too passes and it's on to the next flavor of the month.

Consistency is critical. If you're going to be a hard ass, be a hard ass to everyone. If you're going to ignore people, ignore everyone. Please do not do either of those, hopefully my point is made though. The values, vision and beliefs that organizations share on their website and ones that leadership spit out must be not only shared, but followed. Please don't tell me integrity is a pillar of our value system, then you ask me to leave and adjust our financial report to look better than it is. If an organization and leadership truly want to be a values focused entity, then sharing the difficult news is just as important as sharing the great news. However, by sticking to your values, you have a big team of supporters ready and willing to right the ship.

I remind people sometimes that we do actually control our time and calendar. Sure, we all get requests and meeting invites, but are they critical to what we have to do? Or, can you get a copy of the slide deck and/or notes to be brought up to speed. You just need
to be proactive and committed to controlling your time and calendar. Block off administrative time on your weekly calendar to complete paperwork, respond to emails, organize your 30-60-90-day calendar plan. Have set times to meet with your team and Team Members, set in stone, making them a consistent day/time, let there be no confusion as to when or have overlapping meetings. Schedule training and quarterly catch-ups with everyone together to share what's going on. Check this out, it is OK to decline a meeting if the time slot and/or date does not work for you and may interrupt what you have planned. DO NOT schedule other things over your team and Team Member meetings. This simply lets the Team Member know their time is not important to what you have going on. Things to plan for and have on your calendar:

- Priority work (Your job and/or projects you're a part of.)
- Team and one-on-one meetings
- Professional development/Training
- Lunch and breaks
- Vacations
- Events/Conferences
- Reminders and follow-ups
- Anniversaries and birthdays (For anniversaries, not just the married kind, but Team Members work

anniversaries and business ones. Must celebrate all milestones.)
- Creative and collaboration time (This is time to brainstorm with others over new ideas, projects and to share.)

When we do all of this and do it consistently we begin to build trust with our Team Members. They learn and see that you are holding true to the plan, to the roadmap. That the shared vision established as a team is the priority. This is not the flavor of the month, this is how we do business and succeed.

"A life spent making mistakes is not only more honorable,
but more useful than a life spent doing nothing."
George Bernard Shaw

Chapter 14
Discover the Lessons Learned

I do not believe in reinventing the wheel, but if something isn't quite working right and it seems that a piece is missing or a particular part is broken, then let's explore it and see what's going on. This is where it is so damn important to listen to your Team Members and allow their voices to be heard. If you're a leader surrounded by yes men and women then everything will look wonderful and all the plans will be progressing nicely with amazing results to come, until it all goes sideways leaving you scratching your head and wondering how this could have happened. If you have someone willing to share the truth and not kiss your ass, then these truth tellers should share their perspective of how things are going, how things went in a respectful manner. Helping you to see a clear picture of what is taking place and if any action is needed.

I've sat in meetings with senior leadership after an event or project and everyone is praising one another for the amazing work and achievement, which should be done. We must celebrate our achievements and successes. Unfortunately, that is where it stops and then it is on to the next thing. Then I get to play bad cop, which can be fun at times, but sometimes it's taken the wrong way, even when done respectfully. I love the celebrations, but I love learning from our mistakes too. I love learning why something worked and why it didn't. So, I ask the leaders in the room "What lessons did we learn from this?" I'll ask if they've had an AAR with their teams and when the formal AAR will take place. If one is not scheduled, then let's schedule it. I do this because too often teams repeat mistakes or processes that may work, but are not as efficient and effective as they could be. People are not properly trained or informed on what's to come. An AAR is the opportunity to celebrate and to discover lessons learned.

Identifying lessons learned and having an open and respectful discussion about them is what will make the team and organization even more successful. Lessons Learned are the discoveries we make, the best practices identified and what we should and shouldn't do next time during an event, project or training session. Being able to discuss what went right and wrong and then asking why it didn't go right or why it went wrong. Peeling back the layers to understand at what point did it go sideways. Also, learning why it worked so it can be repeated and improved upon if possible. This extra time used to have an AAR will save you time and money in the long run.

During middle school and part of my freshman year of high school I just could not get algebra down. It was hurting my head and my report card. I was messing up equations and skipping steps that I didn't know I was skipping. None of my math teachers ever shared with me why I was getting things wrong. All I saw were red marks on my homework or worksheets. To be fair, I never asked either, so I am partially to blame for this delay in learning.

Then during my first year in high school I was transferred into Mr. Brozak's class. During his lessons he broke algebra down into segments that made sense. He answered the "why's" that were swirling around in my head and I bet in others' heads as well. He used our examples of incorrect answers to show how it happened, what we missed along the way, what parts we got right and how to correct our actions to get to the right answers next time.

Knowing what I know now, Mr. Brozak was having mini-informal AARs with us and helping us to discover lessons learned. He shared with us, had us share why we did what we did and we learned. It finally clicked. I took back all of the bad adjectives I had used about algebra, though I was not in love with it, I accepted it now. Thank you, Mr. Brozak, wherever you might be.

When we do this as leaders for our Team Members we help them to discover the lessons learned and to better prepare them for future events.

"I like to encourage people to realize that any action is a good action if it's proactive and there is positive intent behind it." Michael J. Fox

Chapter 15
Benefits of an AAR

As a member of the U.S. Army for over twenty-years we used the After-Action Review process before, during and after all events. The AAR was planned for and incorporated into training, deployments and projects whether it was an informal AAR, used to learn on the spot, or a formal AAR that followed immediately after an event was over. A lot of the information I share about the AAR is from the Army's Leader's Guide to After-Action Reviews. During my time in the military I used this and its versions over the years. Now, I've taken what I have learned and removed the military terminology and examples to make it more relatable and understood because it's not just for the military or public service agencies.

During my time working in higher education as an AAR Senior Administrator I reached out to colleagues in other colleges and universities, only to discover that the AAR process is mostly used in their emergency management departments, if they have an AAR process at all, being used as a follow-up to emergencies or natural disasters. While I do understand the use of the AAR in this area, they are missing the opportunity to use all the benefits of an AAR in other areas on their campuses.

The U.S. Army developed the After-Action Review process in the 1970's. They had to address and understand how best to train and prepare for the future. Thus, the idea of learning from what we've done, to improve what we do, led to the After-Action Review. The AAR process asks four main open-ended questions to participants. Guided by a facilitator, participants answer what was supposed to happen, what actually happened, what went right and wrong as well as what to do differently next time.

When these questions are answered, they lead to new questions and answers, the open and respectful discussion leads to discovering lessons learned. Participants begin to understand the "why," and when the "why" is understood, engagement amongst Team Members is higher.

There are many benefits of incorporating the After-Action Review not only in higher education, but in all types of businesses. The first one I'd like to share is that it creates and promotes a culture of learning.

When all participants, regardless of position or tenure with the organization, can respectfully listen and learn another's perspective, it helps to develop understanding. When we can share openly and respectfully, without the fear of repercussions, we can then grow as a team and develop trust.

Another benefit is for leadership and individuals to learn more about their organizational and individual strengths and weaknesses. I'm reminded of the saying, "You only know what you know. And, you don't know what you don't know." This is so true and sometimes fellow colleagues or subordinates just might be embarrassed or afraid to share this.

Fear not though, none of us are perfect and we all have room for growth.

So, whether you do it on your own or with a team, take time to explore and share your organizational and individual strengths and weaknesses. After all, we are all in this together, we succeed as a team.

A few other examples of what an After-Action Review will assist with is identifying problems or missing processes.

The AAR will foster an environment of transparency and accountability, not finger pointing or shining a light on someone who has made a mistake, but simply being open and honest and committing to improvement.

Keep in mind that it is not about solving every problem or coming up with the biggest and best ideas, all that would be great, but simple and small steps to process improvement are just as good.

As the After-Action Review Senior Administrator with the University of North Texas Health Science Center in Fort Worth, Texas, our leadership had a vision and developed a plan that included a focus on process improvement. For a process improvement plan to be successful we must first learn what needs improvement, what's not working and understand the why.

Communication is a vital part of the AAR process and a vital part of any organization that plans to be successful. To have quality communication organizations, leaders and Team Members have to develop a level of professional trust.

Like many things, clear and precise communication needs to become a habit and then it'll be the norm. This includes the sharing of information and experiences. In my research and from speaking with people on my university campus I also learned our departments tend to work in their own silos. The sharing of information and best practices isn't the norm.

This is something an AAR addresses, the sharing of lessons learned and best practice. Since my time in this role I have been fortunate to get positive feedback and Team Members across the campus are embracing this process.

During a cabinet meeting one of the members shared with me prior to the meeting that he included four questions that might look familiar to me in his presentation. Those being the four questions that the AAR addresses, something we'll go over soon.

Sitting in my office working on some AAR notes, another colleague stopped by to share her excitement of the

AAR implementation across campus - she even started using it in her meetings.

Then I received an email from someone I had yet to meet, they were to be a part of AAR training for key leaders in our Texas College of Osteopathic Medicine department. She mentioned incorporating the AAR in her role and that the After-Action Review guide I developed would have been very helpful years earlier.

I think about the Kaizen approach, those familiar with Six Sigma or Lean will know this, it is a proven approach, which means continuous improvement that must be incorporated in your arsenal to achieve cost effective perfection. Though an AAR isn't only focused on being cost effective, more about being people effective and efficient, which leads to cost effectiveness. During an AAR you'll most likely learn about bad purchases or over-priced purchases. That's OK, we learn and we do AARs to prevent repeating mistakes or bad decisions.

The AAR helps to discover potential waste and it also helps to discover all of the great things our Team Members are doing. This cannot and should not be overlooked. These are easy transferable actions for us to incorporate into future events and actions.

After-Action Reviews are designed to help with and even at times remove barriers so the flow of communication, engagement of Team Members and productivity improves. It allows everyone to share their perspective. To speak up and share. When leaders, Team Members and key stakeholders are able to see this impact and understand the value of a quality After-Action Review process the future is wide open.

"To effectively communicate, we must realize that we are
all different in the way we perceive the world and use
this understanding as a guide to our
communication with others."
Tony Robbins

Chapter 16
The After-Action Review

YES! The meat and potatoes of this book! This is
when all the dots start to connect and they form a unicorn.
Ok, maybe not a unicorn, but something just as cool and
lovely. This is when all Team Members and participants get
to share their voice. When leadership should take a seat and
listen.

So, what is an AAR? An After-Action Review is a
professional discussion of a training and/or event that

enables Team Members to discover for themselves what happened and develop a strategy for improving performance and processes.

Organization and teams work with a facilitator that is well versed with the AAR process, the facilitator will provide an overview of the event plan, establish some ground rules, and facilitate the AAR process.

The objective of an AAR is to improve individual and collective performance by providing immediate feedback on actions during or after training and events.

The After-Action Review helps to identify best practices, challenges faced, needed changes to procedures and processes, as well as identify areas for potential professional development.

The AAR's purpose is to assist the organization in achieving its objectives and identify lessons learned so they can be applied to future training or events to improve performance at all levels. Each event is unique and utilizing an after-action review helps to learn from our actions and decisions. In the end, it is about growing as a team and succeeding together.

During an AAR you'll discuss and answer questions to what I call the "Big Four." These are the four steps that make up the AAR. These powerful questions help to open up doors to the discovery of lessons learned. This is the opportunity to have all participants that were involved in the process or event to share their perspective. What it looked like and how it played out through the eyes and actions of all parties which is so important to learning, understanding and better communication.

Here we have my AAR wheel/puzzle (see figure 4). When following these steps and asking open-ended clarifying questions we begin to learn and understand the "whys."

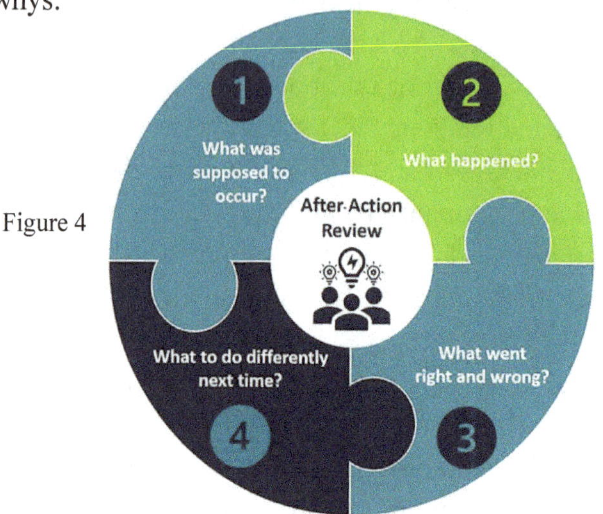

Figure 4

An AAR is about discovery and having a willingness to share openly, honestly and respectfully. We learn from one another when we can have that respectful and professional discussion. Whether it's a formal or informal AAR, both follow the same principle which is to answer the "Big Four."

The first of the "Big Four" questions to answer is **"What was supposed to occur?"** The facilitator, along with the participants, review what was supposed to happen. It's important to learn what Team Members knew or understood about the process. Was the leader's intent, training plan or event objectives clear and precise?

Success begins with understanding and when a plan is communicated well, Team Members understand the "why." Our Team Members are more engaged when we provide clear and precise direction, purpose and motivation. Remember my private story? All he knew was to get on that helicopter and get dropped off at a location that ended up being incorrect. Never assume your Team Members know what is to take place and the why behind it, what is expected of them and that everyone is on the same page. By beginning with this question, we learn how well our plan(s) were disseminated to Team Members. Which can explain a lot in how successful the plan was.

As the discussion progresses, we come to our next question, **"What happened?"** I love a good plan, one that considers all opportunities and challenges. I've spent countless hours in libraries and my office working on plans. Even with all that planning, I know from experience that events can change in the blink of an eye. That's life though and we have to be resilient and adaptable. Getting insight from different stakeholders and participants helps to paint that picture of what actually occurred. This helps everyone engaged to discover lessons learned. It is important for the facilitator to gather as many perspectives as possible. This helps to establish a common understanding of the project/event. Leaders then understand the complexity of an event and work to solve problems quickly if it's on the spot checks or learn to address issues/concerns for future events/projects.

When we begin to discover and learn about how particular parts of an event or project went for others, we start to work our way towards the third question. **"What went right and wrong."** Just to be clear, this is not an opportunity to criticize anyone, this is a time to understand why something went wrong or right. This is an opportunity to understand why the puzzle pieces did or didn't fit. Having a professional and respectful discussion allows participants to open up and share. Regardless of how big or small an error may have been, if an amazing discovery was made or if lunch was late, this is an opportunity to learn. Participants can establish the strong and weak points of their performance based on the leader's intent and performance measures.

The facilitator guides the discussion to ensure maximum input is received, that it is both helpful and relevant to the event. Discovering the right and wrong will help everyone learn why it was done this way or that way. If it was a success, then we want to ensure to capture that and understand how to repeat it. If something didn't go right, it's just as important to capture that information so we learn to not repeat the actions that created it.

As the discovery of lessons learned continues, we find ourselves asking the fourth and final question, **"What to do differently next time?"** Collecting this information is critical, after all the AAR is all about
learning from what we've done to improve what we do. The facilitator guides participants in self-discovery of how the task or tasks might be performed more effectively and efficiently in the future. As a team, participants identify problems, provide solutions and together develop plans for what to do differently next
time. The facilitator guides the organization in self-determining how the task(s) might be performed more effectively and efficiently in the future.

The participants identify problems and provide initial solutions and ideas, as well as identify who is responsible for making the recommended changes. Additionally, the facilitator guides the discussion to determine if there is a more effective way to train the tasks to achieve the leader's intent. This is also an opportunity to confirm what went right and how it'll be continued moving forward and asking ourselves if it can be implemented and duplicated in other areas.

Once the After-Action Review is complete the facilitator will meet briefly with leadership or the project lead to share information and plan for a future follow-up. I like following up with leadership or the project lead so I can learn how the findings from the AAR have been implemented. After all, the After-Action Review is meant to help teams discover, grow and learn. The learning never ends and that's not such a bad thing.

When I have accepted a request to facilitate an AAR I always share my AAR planning methodology (see figure 5). I want the team I am assisting to know my process and timelines.

There are two types of After-Action Reviews, formal and informal. The formal process, which I do 99% of the time, requires more time, resources and all participants of the projects or event are recommended to attend and share.

Leadership should be planning for formal AARs at the same time they finalize their training or event plan (six to eight weeks before implementation). In my university setting, we know the events we are doing year after year. So, the AAR should be scheduled when preparation and planning begins

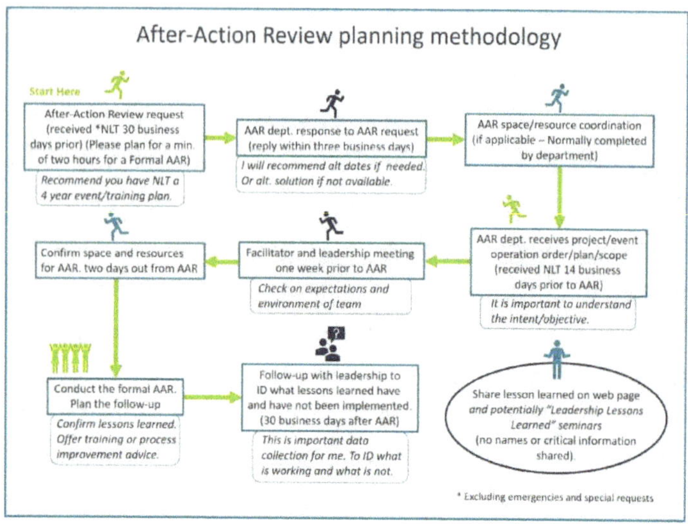

Figure 5

for these events. Formal AARs require more planning and preparation than informal AARs. They require site inspection and selection, deciding which Team Members and external staff is needed, coordination for training and technical support, set up and take down, maintenance/clean-up of the AAR site, depending on what is needed.

Leaders and participants use informal AARs in much the same way as the formal AAR. However, informal AARs can be and should be conducted on the spot. Leaders conduct the informal AAR after previously identified events or as on-the-spot coaching tools while reviewing participants and organizational performance during event(s). Both AARs involve key participants and focus on what was planned, what happened, what did and didn't work and a determination of how to improve performance and increase understanding within the leader's intent.

The information gathered from the informal AARs conducted during events and projects can then be shared with all participants during the formal AAR. This information should be discussed and together we learn the "why" behind the action and changes.

Here is a breakdown showing some of the differences between the two.

➢ Formal After-Action Reviews

- Conducted by a neutral facilitator, should have a note taker and time keeper
- Takes more time to prepare
- Uses more resources
- Thoroughly planned
- Conducted where it can be best supported
- Goes more in-depth into actions or lack there of
- All event/project participants should participate (if available)

➢ Informal After-Action Review

- Conducted by leadership or lead on site of event or project
- Take less time to prepare for
- Uses simple training material that is onsite and readily available
- Conducted as needed
- Primarily based on plan and initial assessment
- Held on site of the event or project

- Opportunity for immediate corrections/feedback and implementation of actions

I am a big advocate for the AAR process, just in case you didn't know that. Bringing together a team or participants in a project or any kind of event can be priceless. It opens the door to so many levels of improvement and opportunity. Whether it be self, team, organization, partnerships or throughout the community and beyond. Discovering lessons learned and then sharing the best practices is just like paying it forward. Helping someone else or another team, providing your insight and lessons learned, to assist them from doing or not doing similar things.

Do not let the AAR process overwhelm you. Sure, it can be in-depth and intense at moments, but stick to the structure of it and take each step, step by step. Have fun in the discovery and be humble. The opportunity to learn is a precious thing my friend. When is doubt, follow these simple steps:

AAR fundamentals (keep these in mind when planning for and facilitating)

- AARs can be conducted during (informal) or immediately after each event (formal).

- What was the leader's intent, training objectives, standards and goal of the event?

- Focus is on all participants and their perspective and

the overall organizational performance.

- Involves all participants in the discussion. Anyone that assisted should have an opportunity to share.

- Use open-ended questions and discover the "why" behind actions.

- Encourages initiative and innovation in finding more effective and efficient ways to achieve standards, meet objectives and the leaders' intent.

- Determines strengths and weaknesses. As a team and individually.

- Links performance to subsequent training. What training is needed moving forward?

- Do not let one person or leadership take over the discussion. Get as many people as possible from different roles involved.

AAR format (the "Big Four" questions)

➢ Ask what was supposed to happen?

- State the event/training objectives and established goals the process was meant to achieve.

- Review with participants what they knew of the plan, scope of work, objective and purpose. What and how much did they know?

- What was each person's, team or department's role in the process? How did it connect to the overall objective/plan?

➢ Ask what actually happened?

- Review what actually happened for a particular event (at all levels). I recommend approaching this chronologically.

- Review actions before beginning the process/step(s). Were participants fully aware of the process and how was it presented/understood?

- Review how the event/training began. Did the event kick off as planned?

- Review reaction of people involved. How did participants interact and work together to achieve the plan/goals?

- Review any changes made to the objective. How did participants react and have to adapt to changes or unintended actions?

- Review events during engagement. How was the process/event perceived?

➢ Discuss what went right and wrong (all levels).

- Review extent to which the team met event/training objectives. Why did it not go off as planned? Why did it work?

- Review extent that the leader's intent was met. How close to the initial plan was work achieved?

- Have participants summarize the major learning points. What lessons did you learn? The good and the bad? The right and the wrong?

- Identify training deficiencies. What additional training is needed for Team Members to better achieve results during future events?

- Identify the organization's ability to perform tasks and meet the leader's intent. What roadblocks did participants face due to the organization's policies and procedures?

- Identify safety risks and measures used to mitigate the risks. Was it a safe and productive environment? If not, why? If it was, why?

➢ Determine how the event or task should be done next time.

- Review extent to which the team met event/training objectives. How was the plan? What needs to change, added or removed to achieve better results?

- Was the leader's or project leader's intent achieved? If not, why? If it was, why?

- Have participants share the major learning points. What lessons have been learned?

- Identify training deficiencies. How can training be completed or incorporated to improve performance?

- Identify the organization's ability to perform tasks and meet the leader's intent. How effective is the team in achieving its mission and goals? What is missing or nor needed?

- Identify safety risks and measures employed to mitigate risks. What safety measure should or should not be taken during the next event?

These examples are merely suggestions and a guide to assist you if needed. The important part is to ask the "Big Four" questions and get participants involved and engaged in the discussion. Keeping it respectful and ensuring it is a safe environment to openly speak.

"Our goals can only be reached through a vehicle of a plan,
in which we must fervently believe, and upon which we
must vigorously act. There is no other route to success."
Pablo Picasso

Chapter 17
Planning for and Executing the AAR

The hard part of the AAR, which should be the
easiest part of it, is planning for it, making it a habit, a part
of all projects, events and training. Plan for it from the start.
If you know a project has a strict deadline of 90-days, then
plan to have the AAR with all participants within two
weeks of completion of the project.

I do enjoy developing fun methodologies (see figure
6) and matrixes, it satisfies the creative in me. It also helps
the visual people that need to see something, hearing the

plan is one thing, but seeing it laid out makes it more realistic and tangible.

You can treat it just like a checklist. I'm sure, at least I hope, you know how wonderful it feels to check off or cross off something you've done and the thrill of knowing it's behind you and you're moving forward with vigor to complete more task/assignments.

To maximize the effectiveness of AARs, formal or informal, leaders must plan and prepare to execute AARs. AAR planning should be a part of all events. Big or small. 300 people or ten people. It does not matter.

Figure 6

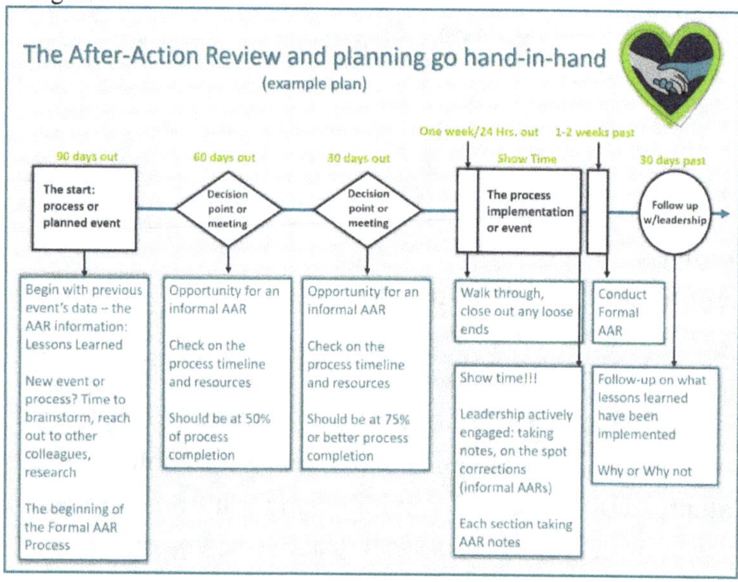

What matters is you and the team are planning to learn and improve. Leaders and Team Members need to understand the organization's mission and its intent overall and for each event. Remember, when we provide direction, purpose and motivation our teams are more engaged, which leads to quality work.

As we plan, leaders or project leads identify opportunities to conduct AARs, coordinate with a facilitator and ensure the allocation of time and resources to conduct AARs are available and ready.

During the event, Team Members and leads should assess the organization, leadership and colleague's proficiency on collective and individual tasks, and complete on-the-spot coaching/informal AARs. Not to catch someone doing something wrong or play "I gotcha!" But to simply correct and improve as we go. This requires that all supervisors understand the leader's intent, concept of operations and task(s) to be completed during an event.

You can be as creative or as simple as you wish to be when planning. The amount and level of detail needed during the planning and preparation process depends on the type of AAR to be conducted and available resources. How much time do you have? Who will be in attendance? How best do your team and participants learn? What kind of environment do you want to create? The AAR planning and execution has four steps(see figure 7):

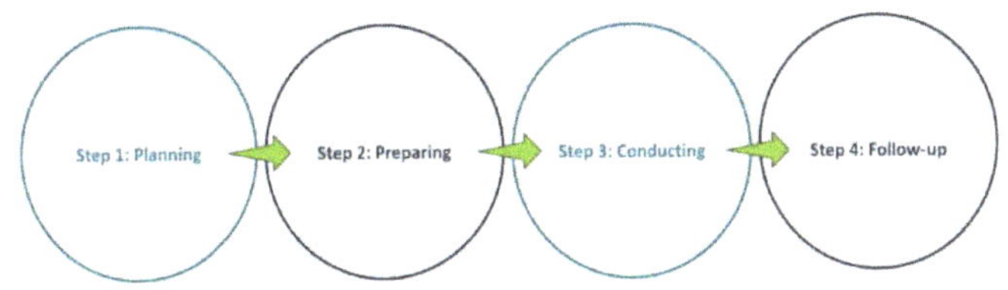

Figure 7

Step 1: Planning the AAR

The AAR plan provides a foundation to build upon and to achieve success, just like any other plan, it's a process to follow to achieve desired results. Leaders provide their intent and guidance to develop an AAR plan for each event. Project leads then determine how to achieve the leader's intent. The guidance applies for formal and informal AARs and should contain:

- Which event(s) are the focus of the AAR
- At what point in the processes of the event are AARs conducted
- Who observes the training and who conducts the AAR
- When and where to have the AAR
- Who should attend and participate
- What resources are needed
- Who is the facilitator, the note taker, the timekeeper

Leaders use the AAR plan to identify critical places and events they must observe, to provide the organization with a timely and valid assessment; examples include organizational maintenance, technical needs and meal breaks/relief. Sometimes you may not be able to have people available to strictly oversee each phase or area of an event. A facilitator may only be available to review the project/event plans and leader's intent. If this is the case, then communicate with your Team Members and have them take notes on critical decisions made, observations and their engagement with participants.

AAR planning includes finding and coordinating, either internal or external to the organization, a person to facilitate the AAR for a particular event. The leader or project leads will oversee the event and it is important to the success of the AAR to have a neutral person act as the facilitator.

When selecting a facilitator keep in mind what is needed and what you expect from a facilitator. They do not need to be subject matter experts on certain business skills you and your team focus on or what the event is about. A good facilitator will ask for and review any and all material prior to the AAR and meet with leadership. They should however, have these attributes:

- Demonstrated proficiency in facilitating an AAR
- Are knowledgeable of the roles and responsibilities
- Have excellent communication, listening and speaking skills

Selection of an experienced facilitator is important to ensure guidance is followed and to maintain a structured professional environment.

❖ Schedule stopping points

Leaders schedule the time and place to conduct AARs as an integral part of events if it is appropriate. Some events may not allow for it. Others, such as a process implementation will allow for scheduled check-in points. When it is allowable, leaders plan for AARs during and at the end of each critical phase or conclusion of major events/milestones. For example, a leader may plan a stopping point after issuing a change to a particular process, when there is a safety concern or after achieving a certain milestone to recognize efforts and Team Members.

❖ Determining attendance

An AAR plan lays out who should attend each AAR. At each level, an AAR has a primary set of participants. At office and department levels, everyone really should attend and participate. At organizational or higher levels, it may not be practical to have everyone attend because of continuing operations or training. In this case, organizational stakeholders, main leaders and other key players may be the only participants. Leaders may request additional participants' participation based on specific observations they're able to share. Should this be the case, those able to participate should complete a team/office AAR prior to such meetings. Bringing with them participants answers to the "Big Four" questions.

❖ Choosing resources and training aids

Training aids can add to an AAR's effectiveness, I recommend only using training aides and resources that will contribute to a successful AAR, rather than for show. Training aids should directly support the discussion of the training and promote learning. Plan and coordinate for the resources that will be needed to achieve a successful AAR and learning environment. Such as:

- Dry-erase boards
- Video equipment
- Digital maps

- Set-up models
- Power and Wi-Fi

❖ Reviewing the AAR plan

The AAR plan is only a guide. Leaders issue their intent, and subordinates determine how to achieve that intent. Leaders and key participants should review the AAR plan regularly during meetings to make sure it is on track and meets the organization's needs. The plan may be adjusted as necessary, keep in mind, changes take preparation and planning time away from others. The purpose of the AAR plan is to allow Team Members as much time as possible to prepare for the AAR.

Step 2: Preparing the AAR

Preparation is the key to the effective execution of any plan. Preparing for an AAR begins before project preparation or training and continues until the actual event. Then it's show time!

Participants must review and understand the leader's intent, event plan, and training objectives before the AAR. It's about knowing your piece of the pie and how it fits into the rest of the pie. Now I want pie. The leader's intent and event/training objectives are the basis for observations and the focus of the AAR. Participants review current processes and procedures, any policies that may be touched on, technical information and applicable SOPs to ensure they have the knowledge and tools to properly observe organization and individual performance.

Based on the leader's intent and organizational objectives, supervisors identify which objective and key results (OKRs) are critical, and make sure they are positioned in the right place at the right time to observe the team's actions, if possible. Otherwise, they may want to inform the team that they will be wanting a complete rundown of events/actions that took place and how teams acted/responded. Examples of important events include:

- Training events that demonstrate OKR proficiency
- On the spot changes to a process or event reorganization
- Contact with outside sources and targeted market
- Needed supplies and personnel change-over
- Participation with the client

AAR facilitators are either internal, participating actively in the event and observing, or external to the department/organization. Reviewing the information collected from the project lead or leadership. Both have the requirement to make and consolidate insights, observations and lessons learned to facilitate the discussion of what happened. Observers keep accurate records of what they see and hear, record events, actions and observations by time sequence to prevent loss of valuable information and feedback. Once again, not an "I gotcha" thing, just capturing their perspective of the process/event.

At times, this may be challenging for leaders actively participating in the event and also facilitating the AAR. But this can be mitigated through professional discussions, feedback and involvement of all participants in the AAR to develop a clear understanding of the event. The observations of all participants during the event not only allow for an understanding of the execution of the task(s) but also the impact of the operational environment. This sharing of observations allows participants and leaders to develop mutual trust through a common understanding of the organization's strengths and weaknesses. We must be willing to communicate respectfully with one another and share our perspectives without fear of retribution.

AARs can occur at or near the event site, it does not matter. What matters is that participants know where and can get there. During formal AARs, leaders identify and inspect designated AAR sites and if needed prepare a site diagram showing the placement of training aids and other equipment. Designated AAR sites also allow pre-positioning of resources and training aids and rapid assembly of key personnel, minimizing wasted time.

During informal AARs, leaders conduct the AAR at or near the event site, on the spot. The difference is that training aids are minimal, if needed at all, and whatever is needed is often found on site. Based on the leader's intent the participants decide on the time and location of the AAR site, if it is not on the spot. Formal AARs should take place no more than two weeks after the event. We want information to be fresh in everyone's mind.

The AAR site needs to be in a location and environment that is comfortable and accessible to all participants. Ensure participants attending the AAR are as comfortable as reasonably possible by removing unnecessary elements and obstacles to learning. This creates an environment where participants can focus on the AAR without distractions.

Leadership or the AAR facilitator can collect observation notes from participants. This helps to develop a picture of what happened during the event, so an effective AAR can be conducted. These notes from informal AARs are important, because they are bridges to on-the-spot changes or corrections and help to clarify why something was done or not.

When organizing the AAR discussion there are several approaches that can be used to achieve results. The facilitator and leadership should consider the options and choose an approach before the session. Such as:

- By key events, themes or concerns

Want to focus on certain areas, then look into a set of themes (client interaction) or events, it may be useful to organize an AAR discussion around key events. For instance, to conduct an AAR for collaborative learning, one might focus on a theme, such as pre-work, the content of the learning sessions, the coaching and reporting and measurement. If implementing a new computer program, you may want to focus on what happened when the program was turned on for all participants/users to use? What were the feedback and trouble points?

- Chronological order of events

When there is not a logical choice of themes or events, a chronological review can be easy to structure and understand. We simply start from the beginning and travel along the timeline. It follows the flow of activity from start to finish. By covering actions in the order they took place, participants may better recall what actually happened when using this process.

- Other approaches

Sometimes an AAR facilitator will employ a blended discussion technique that draws from elements of a chronological and thematic review. Other

approaches a facilitator might integrate include:

- Drilling further into the process or resources behind an event or set of events
- Asking participants to identify unexpected results and discuss their impact
- Collecting data through complementary or more detailed review methods (evaluations, surveys, statistics, etc.)
- Simply asking, "What worked well and what didn't?

As a seasoned AAR facilitator, I rehearse for all of my AARs. It allows me to think of the what ifs. How might participants answer a question or share insight into a particular event. After leadership's or the project lead's planning and after the facilitator has reviewed information, it is about time to put the AAR on the calendar. Leadership will inform all participants when, where and what time the

AAR will take place. Also, I suggest letting participants know what to bring. Mainly, their own perspective and any other resources collected they wish to share. This allows enough time for the facilitator to prepare and rehearse for the AAR while organizational leaders account for personnel and resources and do any preparations on their end.

Step 3: Conducting the AAR

The event is over, pause for celebration, or has reached a stopping point, AAR preparation is complete, and participants are onsite where the AAR will be facilitated. Leadership should share an overview of why they're hosting an AAR. The facilitator shares an overview of what an AAR is, the steps to be taken and together, with the participants, establish the meeting's norms, do's and don'ts. To ensure everyone understands why an AAR is being conducted. The facilitator's introduction may include:

- A polite request for everyone to participate if they have any insight, observation, or question which will help the organization identify and correct deficiencies or sustain strengths. The AAR is a dynamic, candid, professional discussion of training that focuses on organization performance.
  It is a respectful and professional discussion.
- The AAR is not a critique. No one, regardless of position, or strength of personality, has all of the information or answers. AARs maximize learning and understanding by allowing participants to learn from each other.

- The AAR does not evaluate success or failure. Though it may be discussed. There are always weaknesses to improve and strengths to sustain. We are here to discover lessons learned.

Participants participation is directly related to the atmosphere created during the introduction and organizational climate. The AAR facilitator makes a concerted effort to draw in participants who seem reluctant to participate. Don't put them on the spot, but encourage conversation. The following techniques can help the facilitator create an atmosphere conducive to maximum participation:

- Reinforce the fact that it is OK to disagree respectfully
- Focus on learning and encourage people to give honest opinions
- Use open-ended and leading questions to guide the discussion of participants, leaders and organization performance
- Enter the discussion only when necessary
- Encourage people to share only their perspective, do not speak for others

- ❖ What was supposed to happen

The facilitator reviews the leadership team's objectives and restates the events being reviewed, including the conditions and standards. If present, they can use training aides and resources to assist in the AAR process.

The facilitator will guide the discussion to ensure everyone shares what they understand the plan, purpose and the leader's intent was. Have participants restate the events objective/plan and discuss what their part of the process was and how it was planned to go.

❖ What actually happened

As we know plans are wonderful, but even the best of plans may go sideways and we need to be agile and adapt. The facilitator guides participants using either a key event or going chronological through events. The facilitator and participants discuss to the extent possible what actually happened during the event or key processes. Peeling back the onion and asking "why?" Why did the power go out? Why was lunch late? Understanding the why helps to understand and uncover the actions that led to it. The facilitator gathers as many perspectives as possible. This helps to establish a
common understanding. Leaders then understand the complexity of an event and work to solve complex, ill-defined problems for future events and projects.

Perhaps you take a step back and discuss the organization's risk assessment conducted prior to the event and how the participants applied measures to mitigate the risks. This is critical in helping participants understand risk, how they may have acted decisively and determine potential risks in the future.

Dear facilitators, do not ask yes or no questions if possible, but do encourage participation and guide discussions by using open-ended, leading questions. Open-ended questions are also much less likely to put participants on the defensive; these questions are more effective in finding out what happened.

As the discussion expands and more participants add their perspectives, a clearer picture of what really happened emerges. The facilitator does not tell the participants or leaders what was good or bad. The facilitator ensures specific issues are revealed, both positive and negative. Skillful guidance of the discussion will ensure the AAR does not gloss over mistakes or organization weaknesses.

❖ Identify what went right or wrong

The organization must discuss what went right and wrong in the context of the event, objectives and performance measures. To sustain success, the organization needs to know what it is doing well. Also, concentrate on identifying what went wrong and not on the person responsible. Normally if someone did make a mistake it is known. We want to discover the why and the cause, so we can ensure not to repeat the same steps or actions. If necessary, it is better to identify the duty position rather than the person and learn how it could have been performed differently.

❖ Determine how the task should be done differently

The facilitator helps the organization in determining how the task(s) might be performed more effectively and

efficiently in the future. Leadership and participants identify the conditions to modify to
increase the potential for success, challenge leaders and participants to identify opportunities to take advantage of, as well as potential allowable risks within the leader's intent. Additionally, the facilitator guides the discussion to determine if there is a more effective way to train or perform the tasks to achieve the leader's intent. The discovery of lessons learned helps all participants to better understand what to do next time, what not to do, who to include, who not to include and so on.

As the AAR ends, the facilitator reviews and summarizes key points identified during the discussion with the participants and asks any clarifying questions. The AAR should end on a constructive and positive note and link lessons learned to future training/event planning. The facilitator will coordinate with leadership to share their final report and suggestions.

Step 4: Follow-up

AARs are the link between performance and increasing effectiveness as a team and individual. They provide leaders a real life/event assessment tool to plan for Team Member(s) and organizational training. Through a professional and candid discussion of events, participants can compare their performance against the KPIs or job description and identify specific ways to improve.

The benefits of AARs come from applying actionable changes, improvements and in developing future training and event planning. Leaders can use the information to assess performance and to plan future training that will correct deficiencies and at a minimum sustain proficiency. Like I've said, "Train and retain." Questions to ask yourself:

- Have you assessed your training plan?
- What additional training is needed?
- How can we improve overall performance?
- Take time to brainstorm about the previous events and what you would do differently as a team and as an individual. Then develop training for targeted areas and address needs.
- Communicate findings

Because one of the primary goals of an AAR is to contribute to the larger body of knowledge related to an organization's response to various events, a written report that can be shared publicly is the easiest way to communicate the findings to a broad audience.

While a report is ideal, there are additional ways to share best practices, lessons learned, findings and recommendations identified through the AAR. Decision-makers should make every effort to ensure that at least some of the results are shared publicly. Town halls, presentations for relevant stakeholders and department meetings can be effective ways to communicate important parts of an AAR.

- Develop recommendations that are actionable

Recommendations should be actionable and to the extent possible, made with an understanding of the potential implications on budgets and feasibility of implementation. If there are recommendations that will have significant impacts on budgets or be more difficult to implement, an explanation detailing the steps that should be taken or relevant funding opportunities if available should be provided.

Developing a quality AAR that provides specific findings and actionable recommendations will help to provide a blueprint to assist in making any changes and improvements within the department and the organization. Share with external partnerships that may not have been able to participate in the AAR.

- Implement lessons learned (PLEASE)

Finally, an AAR does not achieve its intended purpose until the lessons learned and recommendations have been incorporated back into the department or organization. It is important to ensure that Team Members and leadership understand the importance of this step and champion the recommendations. The AAR can serve as a blueprint for implementing changes to department policy, protocol, culture and training, including to identify which recommendations are priorities.

Assign different strategies to Team Members and get them engaged in the improvement process to make the workplace a more collaborative space.

Whether the changes are implemented directly by the organization and department leaders or an external organization is consulted to provide training and technical assistance based on lessons learned, it is important to identify and implement some, if not all, of the lessons learned and recommendations as quickly as possible to demonstrate commitment to enhancing productivity and the organizational culture. Otherwise, it becomes good old lip service and Team Members will go back to or start thinking all of this hard work is for nothing.

"Education is not the filling of a pot but the lighting of a fire." W.B. Yeats

Chapter 18
Understanding your Team's Learning Needs

When you have completed your after-action review process and you are ready to implement new training or procedures on how to accomplish a certain task(s), then you need to understand how your Team Members best learn. If you've done any research on how adult learners learn, you've discovered they use visual, auditory, kinesthetic and reading/writing styles to develop their brain power and knowledge. Many people use a combination of these four styles, but more times than not, they have a significant style of learning they rely on. It is important that a leader understands this and incorporates a learning needs analysis.

From your after-action review you should have identified areas that need improvement or areas that need a complete overhaul and implementation of new processes and procedures. When these are identified you have to also identify what skills your team and individual Team Members are lacking or need to improve upon. You cannot simply go out and hire a completely new team to check your blocks. We must help our teams and invest in them. So, ask yourself what objective and key results are you wanting your Team Members to achieve? When analyzing this you should answer and assess the follow areas:

➢ Which skills are needed to progress in the organization and for Team Members to excel?
  o Consider company/team goals and what you're lacking to achieve them.
  o Understand your Team Member's perceptions, what do they view as important.
  o Assess your job descriptions for in-demand skills.
➢ What are the Team Member's current skill levels?
  o Measure current Team Member's skill levels.
  o Gather Team Member and peer feedback to support views/plans.
  o Use learning analytics to determine recently developed skills.
➢ Identify what and where the skill gaps are.
  o Determine the gap between current and desired skills.

- o Measure current skills against those needed to progress.
- ➢ How can that gap be closed through learning and professional development?
  - o Establish or update learning resources and identify subject matter experts.
  - o Determine required resources and content providers
  - o Consider content type and how you'll deliver it.
- ➢ Implement a learning development strategy and evaluate the process.
  - o Decide what constitutes success and how you'll measure it.
  - o Assess if the necessary skills are being developed by your Team Members.
  - o Use your learning management system and its analytics.

Think about your organization or team goals and what you're lacking in order to achieve them, think of this as your initial need's assessment. Speak to your Team Members and get their insight into what is missing and any areas they're hoping to improve in.

You can gain valuable insight from current job descriptions in your company and others, provided they are not generic and the same ones have been used since the company opened. Analyze the skills listed and determine if they are relevant, still in-demand in the current job market, and what vision do you have for the variety of roles in your department.

Be transparent and communicate openly with your team. Collect all the feedback and insights, along with your perspective to truly understand the skill and proficiency needed in certain areas. Whichever learning management system you use can be very helpful in assisting you. It should be easy to access and user friendly. Many learning platforms will allow your Team Members to assess themselves and you should include your assessments as well. The learning platform analytics will also be valuable for understanding your Team Member's recently acquired skills. Get engaged in your Team Members professional development. Show you actually care.

No pressure, but this will reflect how well you've conducted the first two stages of your learning needs analysis. Determining the current gap between the skills your team as a whole has, and the individual has now, and the levels wanted/needed to reach your set goals.

At the same time, consider the individual learning and development needs of people in your teams, if you can understand how those align with the organization, you'll be more effective at winning people over. There's a similar situation when it comes to your stakeholders. Their teams will have targets to hit and hurdles to hop over, they'll have their own objectives to conquer and assessing those as part of the learning needs journey will also pull everyone in the same direction.

Start by establishing who are the subject matter experts (SME) when it comes to assessing your existing learning materials. Is there an internal source or will this need to be a contracted external SME? There will be a gap (yes, another gap) between those and the resources you'll need to develop the necessary skills. Creating all of those resources for yourself would be another daunting task, so it's important to use or consider a platform that can curate learning content to cater to the majority of your learning needs.

On the subject of learning platforms, you'll also need to determine how you'll deliver your content and what format will make it most effective, whether that's hands on, webinars, guides, podcasts or a mix. Think of who your audience is. If some of your Team Members are not native English speakers you may need to source additional assistance to translate material. Do any of the Team Members have disabilities that require accommodations? Things to think about.

When you have everything in place and it's been up and running you get to ask yourself and the team, "Are your learning and development practices and professional development pathways developing the necessary skills?" Are you achieving your desired results? Is the team engaged and incorporating the new knowledge? Think about what qualifies as success in this aspect and how will you measure it? This may be influenced by the learning platform or process you choose. If the chosen platform allows you to monitor, measure and assess how your Team Members are engaging with the learning and you can see the return on the investment, then you know you're on the right track.

FYI, it will not be perfect and some Team Members may not like it. You can't please everybody. But, if you can honestly say to yourself, "I'm doing my best and trying to improve things." Then learn from the feedback and improve as you go. Here are some examples of learning needs analysis:

Self-assessment by using journals, log books or weekly reviews. This is an extension of reflection that involves keeping a journal or other account of experiences. However, practice might show that such documents tend to be written nearer the time of their review than the time of the activity being recorded.

Peer reviews involve Team Members assessing each other's performance and giving feedback and perhaps advice about possible improvements, training or strategies to improve performance. Five types of peer review include internal, external, informal, multidisciplinary and Team Member assessment. The last of these is the most formal, involving rating forms completed by selected colleagues and shows encouraging levels of validity, reliability and acceptability.

Observation of a Team Member or department in a work environment performing specific tasks that can be rated by an observer, either according to known criteria or more informally. The results are discussed and learning needs are identified. The observer can be a peer, a senior or a third party if the ratings are sufficiently objective or overlap with the observer's area of expertise.

Critical incident review and significant event auditing technique is usually used to identify the competencies of a profession or for quality assurance, it can also be used on an individual basis to identify learning needs. The method involves individuals identifying and recording, for example, one incident each week in which they feel they should have performed better, analyzing the incident by its setting, exactly what occurred and the outcome and why it was ineffective.

Practice review is a routine review of notes, charts, procedures, letters, requests, etc. That can identify learning needs, especially if the format of looking at what is satisfactory and what leaves room for improvement is followed.

- A few adult learning processes

There are numerous learning processes and you can find resources online, at the bookstore or library when it comes to how adults best learn. Each design, theory or flavor of the month has some quality applications and methods connected with it. Different processes and techniques will resonate better with learners based on their primary learning style. Some of the top learning processes I dug up from my research were:

Andragogy

Andragogy is the "art and science of helping adults learn" and the andragogy theory says that adult learners are different from younger learners in many ways, including:
- They need to know why they should learn something

- They need internal motivation
- They want to know how learning will help them specifically
- They bring prior knowledge and experience that form a foundation for their learning
- They are self-directed and want to take charge of their learning journey
- They find the most relevance from task-oriented learning that aligns with their own realities

Andragogy learning theories focus on giving learners an understanding of why they are doing something, lots of hands-on experiences and less instruction so they can tackle things themselves.

Transformative learning

The transformative adult learning theory (sometimes called transformational learning) is focused on changing the way learners think about the world around them, and how they think about themselves. For example, learners studying religions of the world may gain new perspectives on their principles and thoughts about regions and cultures as they learn more about different religions. Their assumptions may change based on what they learn.

Sometimes transformative learning utilizes dilemmas and situations to challenge your assumptions and principles. Learners then use critical thinking and questioning to evaluate their underlying beliefs and assumptions and learn from what they realize about themselves in the process.

Self-directed learning

Self-directed learning is the process where individuals take initiative in their learning. They plan, carry out and evaluate their learning experiences without the help of others. Learners set goals, determine their educational or training needs, implement a plan and more to enhance their own learning. Self-directed learning may happen online, in the workplace or in the classroom with fellow learners working, by themselves or collaborating as part of their self-directed learning process.

Experiential learning

Experiential learning focuses on the idea that adults are shaped by their experiences and that the best learning comes from making sense of your experiences. Instead of memorizing facts and figures, experiential learning is a more hands-on and reflective learning style. Adult learners are able to utilize this theory and learn by doing, instead of just hearing or reading about something. Role-play, hands on experiences are all part of experiential learning.

Project-based learning

Project-based learning is similar to experiential and action learning in that the overall idea is to actually do something to help you learn, instead of reading or hearing about it. Project-based learning utilizes real-world scenarios and creates projects for learners that they could encounter in their job or future roles. Team Members should be given the opportunity to participate in projects and pursue career objectives they are interested in.

When it comes to adult learners there are many methods they can use to help themselves learn more effectively, including:

- **Setting goals.** Learners who have a specific professional or career goal in mind will have a better experience as they pursue their learning objectives, they have already bought into themselves. You or someone you know may have a goal of learning some helpful conversational Spanish prior to a trip where it would be helpful. As learners we set these goals and know it's in our hands if we succeed or not. If you fail to learn some conversational Spanish, then you'll be left with speaking English in a slow stupid manner, relying on hand and arm signals.
- **Decide why.** Why? Our good old friend. If you know why you need to learn something or complete a degree then success depends upon your actions. Knowing what additional learning will help you to get promoted or advance at work will be the driving reason for you.
- **Review information regularly.** As we get older our brains become less of a sponge and learning new things may not come as easy. Fear not though, you can actually teach an old dog new tricks. You simply need to plan for and take the time to review

new material or best practice. Make it a habit and keep those neurons firing upstairs.

- **Find experiences to help facilitate learning.** Get involved. You don't know something or want to learn more about a particular project? Then volunteer to be a part of it and challenge yourself to become an SME on the topic, or at least dangerously knowledgeable. Work on new projects and collaborate with other Team Members or departments. Step outside your comfort zone and cubicle, find the new challenge.

Using the planning and phases shown in the graphic below (see figure 8), will greatly assist you in making the learning objective successful.

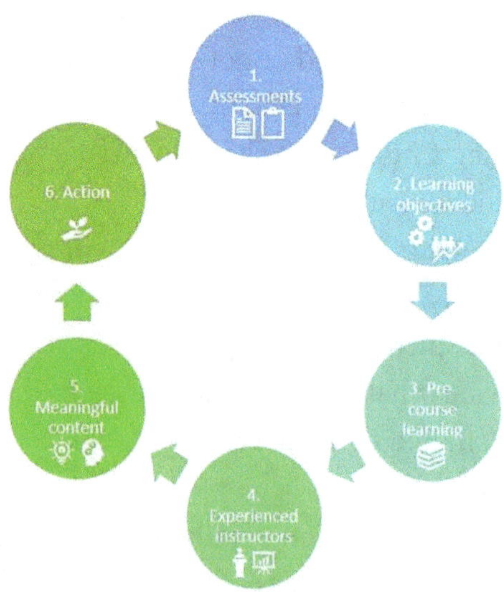

Figure 8

- Assess what training is needed. Where are the challenges and sticking points that my Team Members are continuously facing?

- What is the learning objective? What do my Team Members need to know to excel and do their job proficiently?
- Begin the learning with some pre-course information. Are there any additional reading, online classes and material I can make available ahead of time?
- Ensure your instructor is experienced and presents well. Do they know the subject inside and out? What experience do they have that connects to what my team is doing?
- The content must be meaningful and have a connection to the learner. Is the material relevant? Is the information new and potentially engaging to my team?
- Put the learning into action. PLEASE! A plan without action is just a bunch of alphabets placed on paper that equals a waste of time and resources.

The learning of new information, learning about Team Members, learning the new best practices, learning who's new and what they know, learning what your boss wants compared to needs, learning, learning and more learning. It should never end. It's good for us, personally and professionally.

"If you are going to achieve excellence in big things, you develop the habit in little matters. Excellence is not an exception, it is a prevailing attitude." Colin Powell

Chapter 19
Committed to Service Excellence

Having clearly defined processes and procedures in place is critical to the success of any organization. Regardless of size or type of business, these living and breathing documents help new and old Team Members understand what to do and what not to do. They are a safety net at times, something a Team Member can turn to amongst all the confused noise and say "It's right here in black and white and this is the process." But what if the process isn't working? Or, over the years, accountability has taken a back seat to a dozen other so-called priorities? When this happens, Team Members become frazzled and the perfect storm of stress rains down upon them.

I had the privilege of facilitating an After-Action Review for a team of administrative and business professionals at a medical school in Texas. Unfortunately, they were in the midst of that perfect storm. This particular storm concerned the completion and collection of their residency program's timesheets. A Team Member told me, "The process was like looking forward to a migraine each month."

Along the way the well-intended and what was thought to be a good process become a tangled mess. From faculty not submitting timesheets on time, leaving off valuable hours to some newer administrative Team Members not knowing how many hours their faculty members should be completing each month. It got to a point where the finance team was acting as a middleman. "Houston, we have a problem."

During this particular AAR, though the focus was about the process of collecting residency program's timesheets, it was already known that the process was not working. But it is important to stay the course when facilitating an AAR, do not jump to dessert before you have the main course. Asking the "Big Four" questions (what was the plan, what actually happened, what went right and wrong then what to do differently next time) in order and discovering the why behind actions or lack of along the way is the foundation to the discovery of lessons learned. Those discoveries help to initiate a process improvement plan.

We learn from each participant, their unique experiences and understanding. In this case there was a clear understanding that timesheets were due to department administrators 10 days after the month in which services are rendered and invoices must be sent 30 days after services are rendered. Pretty simple, right? We have due dates and expectations. Everyone participating in the AAR was aware of this. But were the faculty members aware of these timelines/deadlines? Did they understand how to complete them and who to send them to? Did they know the why for it? Or, had they become lackadaisical over time, due to the lack of accountability?

These questions led us to asking, "What actually happened?" As each participant shared, we all learned the answers to those questions, to the best of everyone's knowledge, unfortunately due to schedules there were no faculty members present for this AAR. The collective answers to the questions were a resounding No, No, No and Yes. Thus, leading to faculty members turning in the timesheets late, missing hours or too many hours, all of which are issues. There was confusion with the process. Some department chairs didn't even know the process or what was and wasn't taking place. The initial process had become convoluted. The combination of people not knowing, people not doing, changes in personnel that took the knowledge with them, people going through unneeded channels and all this being time sensitive created that perfect storm.

When we share how things actually went compared to the planned process, it gives us another opportunity to ask why and discover where the hiccups were. These hiccups or choke-points are typically where those not knowing stray. Instead of reaching out for clarification, they simply hit submit or go to the wrong source for information. The participants shared what went right and wrong. Please don't get overly fixated on just the wrong part. Generally, there is just as much that went right and we should carry these things forward as we develop a process improvement plan. No reason to reinvent the wheel. Plus, it saves time and money.

The best thing that went right was that this team was (and is) united and committed to improvement and service excellence. The current process has seen some reduced errors and contracts are getting into the system. It's important to take those victories and build upon them.

Things that went wrong were that not everyone was on the same page or using the same process. Finance should never act as a middleman, and everyone agreed that current faculty and newly on-boarded faculty had to be trained on the process. We don't know what we don't know, never assume someone knows. They needed to understand and know the why. Why it is done this way, why it is important to complete on time and why you must account for and maximize the contracted hours.

When we know the why behind something we are more engaged, we tend to buy-in to a process or plan. With a good why, we are providing direction, purpose and motivation. We are setting our team and organization up for success.

The first three of the "Big Four" questions, as you know by now, set the stage for the final question, "What to do differently next time?" This is when we all get to brainstorm, share ideas, remind ourselves of what went right and how to carry them forward.

Discuss why the mistakes happened and how they can be prevented moving forward. We begin to develop a process improvement plan. Thus, as we filled up sheets of digital paper with ideas and insights, we were easily able to transition into next steps. The "what now?"

For the Team Members that participated in this AAR they knew they had to meet with department chairs, administrative Team Members and faculty, to provide them with guidance, train them on the soon to be new and improved process, and the why behind it. Part of the plan moving forward was to also share the monthly loss revenue and time with chairs and faculty. Helping them to understand better for the "why." Together we developed a clear methodology that everyone could follow. Then, most importantly, was to hold everyone accountable.

Some see accountability as a negative, only used to pressure you to get things done and show you who's boss around these here parts. Not so my friends. Accountability is a good thing. When we have clearly defined roles and responsibilities, we know who to go to for answers or learn where the hold-ups and hiccups are taking place. Then we discover why. It is an opportunity to learn. When Team Members see this in action they are more engaged and feel that their hard work is being noticed and appreciated. It also allows us to train Team Members in need, helping them grow.

This AAR took place in November of 2022 shortly after Thanksgiving. We had scheduled check-ins after that, each of us sharing ideas, new processes and plans to implement. With all AARs I like to schedule 30-and 90-day follow-ups at a minimum. I want to see how the lessons learned are being implemented, how they were received and how I can further assist the team and others that could not attend the AAR. I must say, this team knocked it out of the park. They were committed, they did what they said and said what they did.

I met with the participants of the AAR again in March of 2023. I wanted to learn how the new process was going. A Business Coordinator for Educational Programs with the medical school said, "The old process was frustrating, confusing, and really time-consuming." She shared some statistics with me and my mind was blown away!

From January of 2022 to Aug of 2022 the overall percentage of timesheets, being late and/or not maximizing hours was 86%.

From August to November of 2022 it was 71%. Both are staggering and sad percentages to see. For fiscal year 2022 lost revenue was a big issue and over 300 hours went unreported.

In the time since our AAR and process improvement planning that number has shrunk to 14%. Not perfect, but still lovely to see. Afterall, we strive for perfection, but succeed with improvement. Improve they did!

This is a testament to leadership empowering Team Members and Team Members taking action to improve the workplace. When we work together, learn from what we've done to improve what we do and communicate well, we can achieve greatness.

The power of the AAR is to give a voice to all participants. In this case, some participants were not able to attend the formal AAR. But a plan was implemented to bring them up to speed and I also made myself available for questions, chats, and provide clarification and guidance if needed.

This is only one example of the success and benefits of utilizing the AAR. Whether it's a small project or bigger one, such as this, taking the time to communicate openly and respectfully is critical to the success and well-being of all members of the team, at every level.

"I have learned that as long as I hold fast to my beliefs and values - and follow my own moral compass - then the only expectations I need to live up to are my own."
Michelle Obama

Chapter 20
Woo, That's a lot of Stuff!

A lot of information is presented to you in these pages. If you've been a good learner, you have committed what you've read thus far to memory. If not, read again. LOL! Just kidding. Don't let improvement in the workplace, life place or any place overwhelm you. All we can do is our best and we can hope, though hope is not a strategic plan. To make significant impactful changes for the greater good of all, to work well and play well with others we have to put in the effort.

Remind yourself and if need be, others that you are not studying for the next big exam or attempting to change our unique tax or presidential voting system. You are simply doing your best to improve yourself and the workplace. If you can improve upon one aspect of them, then rock on with your bad self! It takes time, it's a process and it is work. Yes, that other four-letter word we so dearly love. Work though, can be rewarding and just as fun to say as the other four-letter word. For me, work has become a synonym for achievement and positivity. I strive to have an impactful day where I can achieve set goals, help others, and that the work I do will have a positive impact for others.

Setting goals for yourself and team is important, it helps to build a culture of success and learning. What training or changes do you want to implement this quarter, pick one and be its champion. Then repeat the process for next quarter and the following two. When the year is over, take a step back and review what you've done and review with the team. I like to call it an After-Action Review, go figure. Taking the time to answer the "Big Four" questions will help you and the team to discover the lessons learned, the good ones and the "let's not do that again" ones.

When we plan and take things step by step, things tend to be less overwhelming, and our stress levels do not have to go haywire. After all, how many things can you really do at one time? Walk and chew gum? Even as I type this, I had to stop for a brief few seconds to take a sip of coffee. Not something I would try to knock out while typing. Fact is multi-tasking is BS. Because in reality you are still only doing one thing at a time at any particular moment. Once a task is completed for a particular project you may jump to another project and knock out a task for that. But you're still only doing one thing at a time. So be easy on yourself and simply do one thing at a time, as best as you can.

There is a lovely book out on the market by Gary Keller along with Jay Papasan called "The One Thing" and I highly recommend it, which means nothing, but read it anyway. It's about achieving extraordinary results by focusing on one thing. It's full of wit and common sense. Most importantly it clearly shows how a very successful person focuses on the current one thing that is most important. Check this out… Gary even blocks off time on his calendar to do some self-development! WTH! As I have said, plan for your professional/self-development, especially if it's work related and will significantly contribute to your success in the role you are currently in or working towards.

One thing I must add in here, other people's emergencies do not constitute it to be an emergency for you. Many of those so-called emergencies are due to piss poor planning and/or stepping all over their calendar and trying to book multiple things at the same time back to back to back with no time between. Literally, their calendar has zero free minutes in it to breathe. Geez, why are you so stressed? DUH!

I'm not saying don't assist, but do not let it be a distraction for you or mess up your planning and workflow. Yes, there will be actual emergencies that arise, that's life and we humans are wacky. When you are not stressed you are able to be more agile and adapt to needed changes. Your deodorant is working well and you continue to flow like a lovely river.

"Passion is one great force that unleashes creativity, because if you're passionate about something, then you're more willing to take risks." Yo-Yo Ma

Chapter 21
The Power of Creativity

I share this section because we have to be creative in what we do. It is how we discover better ways of achieving something. It's how we learn to get the best out of our Team Members and it helps to ignite our creative networks in our brains. 60% of polled CEOs say that creativity in the workplace is seen as an important leadership quality (thrivemyway.com 2023). However, are leaders allowing their younger leaders and Team Members the opportunity to be creative? Or is it an atmosphere of just getting it done, no time for creativity. Another stat from Thrive My Way (2023) lists that 35% of workers say that they are only given a few times a year to be creative at their place of work.

All too often I hear people say, "I'm not creative," or "I wish I was creative like you," we then end up in a conversation about creativity. Discussing our likes, our favorite artists, and then the past comes into play with a few sad words "I used to…." So now it's not a matter of you aren't, but you need to get back into the groove, make time, and get those creative juices flowing once again.

You're probably saying to yourself, "easier said than done" and I agree. It is easy saying "easier said than done" and it is also easier typing it than doing it. Success and rewards do not simply show up for those that are not willing to put in the effort. They present themselves when you've put in the effort. In a professional environment, we have to decide when we can be more creative. It depends on the scope of work, the team assembled, time and even costs. Plus, what kind of workplace are you a part of? Working in higher education allows me to be more creative in what I do. When I was working with other organizations my creative leash was relatively short.

Let me first clarify the kind of creative success and awards I'm talking about. There are many awards given, such as participation, attendance, and volunteering. Just as success can be in completing a project on time, accomplishing a goal and so on. These are nice. Let me add in, it shouldn't be about the money. Trust me, I do enjoy getting paid for what I do, but there are some things I'd do for free, because I do it for me. Money will find a way of leaving your hands, wallet, and/or bank account in due time.

My kind of success and award is when I see a plan achieved and the team's excitement. When a new Team Member is able to fly on their own, when different departmental silos break down and communication flows like a river and even when a piece of art I've created is hanging on someone else's wall. Those kinds of successes and awards will be lasting memories you can share for many years and are priceless.

We are all creative in our own way and should have fun with it. Some may be the kind of artist that can rebuild a car engine like Rembrandt paints - making it look easy. Others I've seen convincing people to purchase things, like the Robert Frost of the sales world. All those doctors out there that understand how to operate on people, carving like the great Auguste Rodin. Ok, enough of the examples. There are three distinct brain networks that are the key to most creative thinking. These are known as the executive control network, which activates and operates when a person needs to focus. The default network, which is related to brainstorming and daydreaming. Then finally the salience network, which is for detecting environmental stimuli and switching between the executive and default brain networks (The Neuroscience of Creativity, T. Patnaik, 2/2021).

The point is we simply do not recognize our creative skills, we overlook them and think of them as work or "that's just something I do", DUH! And you do it well.

Giving ourselves credit for the abilities we have isn't bragging, it's who we are, and we need to applaud ourselves and the abilities we have once in a while.

When I am working and assisting others, I love being able to ask why and peel the layers back to discover each layer of why and the actions taken. This helps the participants to visualize and get those creative juices flowing. They start to think of other actions that may have been more effective and efficient. Realizing that just because something has been done the same way ninety-nine times doesn't mean it can't be improved upon.

I highly recommend when facing a new challenge and working on a project, you take a step back to reflect and to turn off. Work life isn't going anywhere, the busy and hectic world will wait for you. We must take an occasional time out and do something else. Just to let another part of the brain relax while you rejuvenate yourself. Write, paint, draw, build, or bust out the coloring books and color. Do a puzzle for five minutes. Give yourself a break and some time to refresh (set a timer if time is critical).

I see many job postings that tag innovation, adaptability and even productivity as key traits an employer is looking for. To have those three traits is to allow your current and new Team Members to be creative. They go hand in hand. 3M, which creates SO many things, has an awesome thing called "15 percent time." They allow Team Members to use a portion of their time to brainstorm and to pursue their own passion projects. In 1974, Art Fry invented the iconic Post-it Note during his "15 percent time," I think we all know how iconic the Post-it note has become. So, leaders, let your people get creative for a bit. Team Members, ask for some creative time, plan for it. You don't have to invent the Post-it notes on day one. Just let your ideas flow.

No complex thinking involved for now, just create, and see where it goes. You just might surprise yourself and discover the missing pieces or needed steps to your process. Then, when you have to get back to work, you'll feel relaxed and I bet even have a few more creative ideas about handling certain projects, people or a new invention.

"I thank life for teaching me how to be sarcastic. It's funny how it keeps me humble and humored."
Brendan T. Kelly

Chapter 22
Final Thoughts

Well, I hope all these alphabets strategically placed side by side to form words and the delicately and brilliantly way they aligned with one another to form sentences made you think, laugh, complain, take-action or any other response for that matter. After all, this book was from my perspective and shared experiences. The collection of experiences through life, work, love, humor and attempting to understand why will lead you down your own unique path. As you implement the AAR and begin to discover lessons learned, you too will want to laugh, cry and scratch your head and wonder "WTH?!"

"Why?" Can be one heck of a question to answer. Some people spend their life attempting to answer it. One darn word! Why? It drives us. It excites us. It makes us ponder. Yes, it even makes us angry. But, at the heart of it, somewhere deep within those three letters lies the heart of it all. A desire, a wanting, a need for us as human beings to understand what is going on, how it happened and what we can do to make it better.

I doubt a gazelle that just got taken down by a lion is asking why. Why me Mrs. Or Mr. Lion? Nope, most likely they are thinking "DANG! I got got! How can I escape…" then silence.

We wacky human beings with this incredible mind need to know and need to know it all. We want the details and how those details or plans will pertain to us. Even the unengaged Team Member wants to know how something pertains to them and they'll think to themselves "How will this mess up my flow of looking busy?" "I am leaving at 5:00:00 PM no matter what!" I wonder when, at what point in all of humanity, did mankind start to wonder why? I'd be willing to bet that the earliest of mankind from some 200-300 thousand years ago didn't ask why. They acted much like the animals and simply survived. Which included kill or be killed. Eat, drink, rest and so on. Or is why something that is automatically built into us from birth? My kids somehow learned to ask why over and over again.

Whatever the case or thinking it entails, we simply have a passion to understand the why. That in my opinion is good. Best used when asked prior to a potentially dangerous action. Don't ask why after you've watched someone mix bleach and ammonia together to get that deep cleaning on of their floors. Ask why before that "Why are you holding those two bottles and looking like you're about to pour them into that bucket?"

The same "why" can be asked and should be asked if we're about to repeat the same process that has failed us multiple times before. When does the insanity stop!? NASA has a wonderful program called PaL (Pause and Learn). Their Pause and Learn sessions are structured discussions that focus on recent project developments, challenges, and critical milestones. An opportunity to identify what is going right and wrong, what is needed to correct or continue progress and to learn. I love it! It is their version of an AAR. At each benchmark they are taking time to discover the lessons learned.

Planning and getting your Team Members and colleagues involved, having open and respectful communication, taking time to learn from actions/events is a wonderful opportunity to learn. We should not ignore an opportunity to learn, sharing what we've learned to those that could not attend. When we give our Team Members a voice at the table, we are allowing our team to grow and exceed our established expectations. By empowering everyone to share we create one heck of a culture that is focused, consistent and capable of achieving anything.

Enjoy and be well.

Let's connect.
Instagram: @brendankellyaar
LinkedIn: www.linkedin.com/in/brendan-t-kelly/
Webpage: https://brendankellyaar.wixsite.com/my-site

Brendan Kelly is an expert at facilitating After-Action Reviews and training groups on the topic. Along with his MBA, he is also a Lean Six Sigma Black Belt, a Certified Change Management Professional and has a passion for helping teams and individuals succeed. Brendan served in the U.S. Army for 22 years. Upon retirement he worked as a High School Teacher teaching Leadership Education, oversaw recruiting and retention programs in the private sector, Created the first After-Action Review Department in High Education at the University of North Texas Health Science Center (an achievement he is very proud of). Currently Brendan works with the State of California as a Performance Development Consultant. Brendan says "What keeps me going is a desire to help others, improve team dynamics and helping an organization become more efficient and effective. When we can do this, we grow as a team, barriers come down, communication improves, people are more collaborative and engaged." Brendan has been nominated and received many awards over the years. From Soldier of the Year to Teacher of the Year.

The power of "A Voice at the Table" is that it shares real world experiences, data and insight into the benefits of giving each person a voice, an opportunity to be heard. Respectfully communicating with one another and learning from each other. When we actively listen to all of the experiences of those we interact with on a daily basis we are building a culture of respect and collaboration. The After-Action Review allows for each perspective of an event or project to be shared, discussed and even respectfully debated. It gives everyone a voice at the table.

You can reach out and connect with Brendan on Instagram @brendankellyaar.